THE SPIRIT
IN PUBLIC
THEOLOGY

4-13-11 - W
from Ollie's)

Larry Thompson

THE SPIRIT
IN PUBLIC
THEOLOGY

Appropriating the Legacy of Abraham Kuyper

Vincent E. Bacote

B
Baker Academic
Grand Rapids, Michigan

Published by Baker Academic
a division of Baker Publishing Group
P.O. Box 6287, Grand Rapids, MI 49516-6287
www.bakeracademic.com

Printed in the United States of America

Library of Congress Cataloging-in-Publication Data
Bacote, Vincent E., 1965–
    The spirit in public theology : appropriating the legacy of Abraham Kuyper / Vincent E. Bacote.
        p.   cm.
    Includes bibliographical references and index.
    ISBN 0-8010-2740-3 (pbk.)
    1. Kuyper, Abraham, 1837–1920. I. Title.
BX9479.K8B33 2004
261′.1—dc22   2004013961

CONTENTS

PREFACE

This project stems from an effort to discover and articulate a valid theological rationale for Christian engagement in the public realm. This endeavor stretches back to my pre-seminary days. Before I began to pursue my Master of Divinity degree from Trinity Evangelical Divinity School in 1990, I was troubled by what appeared to be a lack of theological argumentation for Christian public engagement. In my experience with the parachurch organization the Navigators and the subculture of American evangelicalism, I had been exposed to approaches to Christian living that strongly emphasized the distinction between Christians and "the world." In this approach to Christian living, engagement in cultural activity was encouraged only if the public activity was distinctly Christian. This meant that the activity had to have objectives that were either evangelistic or aimed at spiritual edification. In addition, there was a skeptical attitude toward the value of endeavors such as political action and other forms of societal engagement. This state of affairs was frustrating to me because I perceived myself to be a "culture-affirming" person who saw things in society and culture as worthy of appreciation and involvement.

Near the middle of my time at Trinity, two professors directed me to the topic of theology of culture and public life and introduced me to the work of a Dutchman named Abraham Kuyper (1837–1920), especially his Stone Lectures on Calvinism. Reading Kuyper's text on theology of culture was like breathing some much needed oxygen.

Though Kuyper was not a perfect figure (his problematic view of race is a glaring example), I was drawn to his vision of Calvinism as a life system that encouraged and even demanded public engagement. In the Stone Lectures, Kuyper presented the doctrine of common grace as the impetus and rationale for Christian involvement in every aspect of the created order. In reading about this doctrine, I encountered for the first time a Christian affirmation of creation. Though Kuyper used language about the fall, it did not lead him to fatalism. Instead, he highlighted the fact that the world was not chaotic and that Christians had a responsibility to develop the potential latent in creation. I resonated with Kuyper's call for Christian action in the world in every realm.

I discovered that Abraham Kuyper was a remarkable man. In the Netherlands, he helped found the Anti-Revolutionary political party and the Vrije Universiteit of Amsterdam, edited weekly and daily newspapers, served the church at both the local and the regional level, and was the prime minister of the Netherlands from 1901 to 1905. His life embodied his theology of culture and politics.

Kevin Vanhoozer suggested that I look for a relationship between pneumatology (the doctrine of the Holy Spirit) and Kuyper's theology of culture. I read Kuyper's book on the doctrine of the Spirit and there discovered that the language used to describe the work of the Spirit in creation was similar to Kuyper's description in the Stone Lectures of the function of common grace. The connection between pneumatology and common grace is the baseline for the issues addressed in this book. I first wrote about this connection in a presentation I gave to the Systematic Theology Group at the 1996 annual meeting of the American Academy of Religion. The presentation was titled "Called Back to Stewardship: Recovering and Developing Abraham Kuyper's Cosmic Pneumatology" and was later published in the *Journal for Christian Theological Research*. This book significantly expands the ideas found in that article. In particular, this book articulates a larger vision of common grace and the work of the Spirit in creation and attempts to provide a better understanding of Kuyper's brand of public theology.

It is necessary not only to understand what Kuyper has said but also to recontextualize his approach to pneumatology and public theology in light of the current era. A coherent recontextualization of Kuyper's pneumatology and public theology provides a way to bring his insights into the present and to lay a foundation for further use of his work in the decades to come. This is necessary if the present book is to be more than an excursion into the past.

In the area of pneumatology, I was particularly interested in interacting with authors who had addressed the role of the Spirit in creation and had reflected on the resultant public implications in areas such as cultural development, the environment, and politics in general. This is not a typical approach to pneumatology, especially within the evangelical circles with which I am familiar. While Pentecostalism, the charismatic movement, and the Third Wave brought considerable attention to the doctrine of the Holy Spirit in the past century, the focus in the majority of works on pneumatology, or in appropriate chapters in works of systematic theology, is on the work of the Spirit in soteriology. More specifically, the prominent issues revolve around arriving at a better understanding of the manner in which the Spirit applies the redemptive benefits of Christ to believers.

Here, my focus is on the work of the Spirit in creation in a manner that is not explicitly redemptive but that provides a reason for Christian engagement in society. While it is always wise to ponder anew the manner in which the Spirit redeems individuals, it is equally important to understand and bring to light the manner in which the Spirit's work in creation prompts responsible engagement in all spheres of the world, from politics to culture to environmental ethics. Put differently, I am seeking a way to address the relationship between the Spirit and nature and to arrive at a theological foundation for prudent interaction with the created order. This pneumatological inquiry has led me to consider an approach to understanding the doctrine of creation that is distinct from the issue of origins and to examine the relationship between creation and history.

In contemporary thought, figures such as Jürgen Moltmann, Geiko Müller-Fahrenholz, and Mark Wallace particularly represent the strand of my research that reveals current approaches to the relationship between pneumatology, the environment, and sociopolitical engagement. The question of how the Spirit's work in creation yields a particular approach to the natural world is of vital importance, especially because environmental concerns are prominent in the current sociopolitical climate. Colin Gunton, Clark Pinnock, and Sinclair Ferguson articulate important approaches to the Spirit's work in creation, though they offer less reflection on sociopolitical and cultural implications. John Bolt of Calvin Theological Seminary introduced me to Arnold A. Van Ruler, the primary dialogue partner in the fourth chapter. I found in Van Ruler a figure who provided me with the necessary categories for developing a distinctly pneumatological perspective on the Spirit's work in creation. Though his work is soteriological in focus, it fit my interest in creation and could be utilized to contemporize Kuyper's doctrine of the Spirit in creation.

The scope of public theology is also limited in this volume. Public theology investigates issues such as the potential for theology to serve as a form of public discourse and the development and explication of a theological motivation for public engagement. While certain prominent figures in the evangelical world have encouraged considerable public involvement in the last two decades (from culture wars to political issues), there has not been an adequate theological rationale for this foray into politics and culture. This can be attributed to certain forms of pietistic thinking that bring great focus to issues such as the personal morality of public figures but do not adequately give reasons for involvement in the political process or in cultural development. In particular, the apocalyptic eschatology that yields a negative view of the created order can lead to considerable confusion regarding theological reasons for engaging society. After all, if the world is getting worse and worse and will end soon, what valid reason is there for public engagement apart from saving individual souls? In this book, public theology is related to a view of creation that acknowledges fallenness without the necessity of a fatalistic view of public engagement. I believe that society can actually improve as a result of a sound public theology.

This work focuses on approaches to public theology that can be labeled "apologetic" and "confessional." Apologetic approaches involve ways to dialogue with those who are not Christian, while confessional approaches emphasize distinctive Christian approaches to politics and social order. A significant question addressed here concerns the proper categorization of Kuyper's public theology. This is a challenge because of the episodic nature of Kuyper's public theological essays and activities. Chapters 2 and 3 reveal that both the apologetic approach and the confessional approach resonate with Kuyper's public theology. Furthermore, these two approaches provide categories that may bring clarity of understanding, as Kuyper scholars and other critics have expressed frustration and confusion over the apparent inconsistency in the theological rationales given by Kuyper for public engagement.

Notable by their absence are various forms of political theology. Latin American liberation theology, black theology, and feminist theology are all forms of public theology that intend to give voice to marginalized groups and promote sociopolitical change. To varying degrees they reflect the ideologies of Marxism, postmodernism, and other intellectual and social frameworks that are explicitly public. While it is true that Kuyper was concerned about the public representation, engagement, and impact of a marginalized constituency in the Netherlands, his public theology often opposed the ideologies represented by these alternate theologies. If the intent of this book were to change radically Kuyper's public theology or to recast it as a theology of socialistic activism, then it would be not only appropriate but also necessary to include these political theologies. Since it is my intent to arrive at a clear understanding, categorization, and slight modification of Kuyper's public theology in the spirit of neo-Calvinism, it is best to limit this work to the areas of apologetic and confessional public theology.

My hope for this work is that it will provide a contribution in three main areas. First, I would like it to provide insight into Abraham Kuyper studies. In the United States, Kuyper is understood as a man of ideas, and in the Netherlands, he is primarily a historical figure. Though this work focuses primarily on Kuyper's ideas, the man of history is present, particularly in the evaluation of his public theology. Hopefully, this work will provide not only greater exposure of Kuyper beyond church and academic circles of Dutch heritage but also greater understanding of this complex man.

Second, I would like this book to contribute to the field of pneumatology. A fully trinitarian theology requires that the work of the Spirit be distinguished in all areas, not just soteriology. The nonredemptive work of the Spirit in creation is important and requires theological reflection and articulation. Furthermore, it is important not only to reflect on the Spirit's work in creation but also to reveal the direct relationship between cosmic pneumatology and public theology.

Public theology is the area in which I wish to make a third contribution. By extending the idea of public theology to the stewardship of the entire created order, I hope to begin the development of a public theology (primarily in the evangelical world but also beyond) that will prompt greater numbers of Christians to move beyond life in a Christian enclave. If Christians are involved responsibly in arenas other than the church or explicitly Christian organizations, we will see the development and emergence of a society that is beneficial to everyone. This desire is much like that of Kuyper, who envisioned a world structured according to the ordinances of God. It is true that the Netherlands scarcely resembles Kuyper's vision, but the failures of his followers provide me with caution, not disillusionment. I realize that it will take more than the words of this book to bring about my lofty vision, but this is where I begin, and it is a long way from the frustrations I faced before entering seminary in 1990.

ACKNOWLEDGMENTS

The process of writing a dissertation and revising it for publication was the occasion for me to benefit from the influence of many individuals. The members of my dissertation committee provided me with invaluable input as I pursued the completion of my degree. Donald Dayton offered me numerous challenges and insights that broadened my view of theological tradition and added a unique shape to my understanding of the Reformed tradition. Max Stackhouse has been a valuable guide and mentor in helping me understand the relationship between theology and public life, and I am grateful for his input. Dale Irvin is a valued friend and was a helpful resource throughout my entire tenure at Drew University, and his engagement with church history and various theological traditions has helped me understand the heritage of Christianity with much greater depth. I am thankful for such a helpful group of mentors.

I am grateful for the assistance provided by George Harinck, Cornelis van der Kooi, and D. Th. Kuiper when I visited the Netherlands three times while undertaking this project. They and others I met in Holland gave me insight into Abraham Kuyper and his world in invaluable ways that made this book much better.

I also thank Wheaton College for providing the means to travel to the Netherlands to accomplish the bulk of this revision. Nathan Smith provided superb help as my research assistant, performing a variety of tasks and serving as a discussion partner during a trip to the Netherlands.

My parents, James and Vermell Bacote, have always been very supportive of me, throughout my entire graduate education and beyond. I am thankful to them for standing behind me all these years and saddened that my dad did not live to see this book appear in print. Finally, I thank my wife, Shelley, and my daughters, Laurel and Juliana. Shelley moved from Chicago to the strange forest of Drew University two months into our marriage, took jobs she did not always find pleasant, and supported me in spite of the unique challenges she faced while I finished my education. She later endured several weeks without me when I went abroad to revise my dissertation. Her patience, love, and support are worth more than I can express here, and my two daughters have provided their father with countless moments of joy amid the hard work of completing this book.

I

WEAVING THE THREAD

Three strands comprise the thread that runs through this volume. The first deals with key themes in the doctrine of the Holy Spirit as it is related to creation (understood as nature or the biophysical order, with implications for history). The second is public theology, particularly in reference to articulating a theological rationale for Christian public engagement in every sphere of life, ranging from politics to the arts. The third is the work of Abraham Kuyper (1837–1920), the Dutch figure who simultaneously served his church and society as a theologian, politician, journalist, and ecclesiastical leader. The study of these themes and diverse approaches to them requires clarity about the method used, beginning with the approach to systematic theology that stands behind it.

SYSTEMATIC THEOLOGY

This book is an exercise in Christian systematic theology, the discipline that attempts to interpret and articulate the meaning, coherence, and implications of Christian claims. Systematic theology draws on other disciplines such as historical theology, philosophy, and biblical studies but is distinct from them in its aim to present a synthetic, coherent, and contemporary picture of the faith. Methodologically,

15

this book attempts to articulate Kuyper's theological perspective and
the core theological issues and themes involved, with some reference
to the ideas that underlie his theology, and to engage in constructive
theological dialogue. The theological dialogue aims at a contemporary restatement of Kuyper's theology by virtue of engagement with
contemporary thinkers and theological reflection. Readers should not
perceive the term *constructive* to imply an exercise in imaginative
and fanciful theological speculation but an attempt to articulate a
coherent and contemporary statement of the relationship between
the work of the Holy Spirit in creation (or "cosmic" pneumatology)
and public theology. Like Kuyper's work, this restatement and recontextualization is comprised of biblical, philosophical, and historical
and contemporary theological elements, and it aspires to be faithful
and relevant for the present age.

CREATION AND HISTORY

Those who work on issues of public theology often draw on doctrines of creation. However, under diverse influences such as Karl Barth
and dispensational theology, much reflection on creation has focused
on God's redemptive intent in Jesus Christ from the beginning. While
this is a valid and extremely important emphasis, this book aims, in
contrast, to articulate a coherent expression of the Holy Spirit's work
in creation. It does so not to set creation against redemption but rather
to direct greater attention to creation in Christian theology. With this
focus, how is creation to be understood? In theological discussions,
the term *creation* often refers to the issue of the origins and causality
of the created order. In another theological use, the term refers to the
biophysical universe (seen as a result of divine causality) in which we
live.[1] In this book, creation is primarily understood in the second sense
and can also be understood as nature or the natural world. While
creatio ex nihilo is assumed in this book, and while the relationship

1. A book that engages both of these definitions is Colin Gunton, ed., *The Doctrine
of Creation* (Edinburgh: T & T Clark, 1997). It focuses primarily on issues related to
the first definition of creation, but it does contain references to the second definition.
Jürgen Moltmann, *God in Creation: A New Theology of Creation and the Spirit of
God,* trans. Margaret Kohl (Minneapolis: Fortress, 1993); idem, *The Spirit of Life: A
Universal Affirmation,* trans. Margaret Kohl (Minneapolis: Fortress, 1992); and idem,
The Source of Life: The Holy Spirit and the Theology of Life (Minneapolis: Fortress,
1997) make explicit reference to creation as the biophysical order or as nature.

between divine creativity and human creativity underlies aspects of the discussion of public theology found in this work, the central idea is that the Holy Spirit's preserving (and providential) presence in the biophysical order encourages (invites, prompts, spurs) stewardly engagement of the created order (manifested in ways such as cultural development and political involvement). From a Reformed perspective, this is viewed as a broad-ranging fulfillment of the cultural mandate found in Genesis 1:28 and a reflection of the implications of the Noahic covenant in Genesis 9:1–17.[2] While, as Colin Gunton notes, the doctrine of creation is indeed concerned with the interaction of the eternal God and the world he has made,[3] it primarily concerns the constituting of the world at its advent. This book concerns divine involvement in the world "already made" and the subsequent human response of engagement and development.

A difficulty arises when one considers how it is that culture and politics are manifestations of stewardship of the biophysical creation. In one sense, this question is answered by showing the link between creation and history. Put simply, history is the horizon of human activity.[4] The relationship between creation and history is important because it provides a way to speak of the significance of acts on the divinely created biophysical order while keeping it distinct from a discussion of creation as the product of divine causality.[5] Here

2. The cultural mandate is a Reformed interpretation of Genesis 1:28–30. The created order requires development, and humans serve as coworkers who carry on the work of the world. While God's creating work is finished, the world is in a state of potentiality, requiring the work of humans (created in the divine image) to develop the earth toward the realization of this latent potential. Governance, family nurture, daily labor, and marriage are among the tasks of the cultural mandate. For a good summary, see Gordon Spykman, *Reformational Theology: A New Paradigm for Doing Dogmatics* (Grand Rapids: Eerdmans, 1992), 180–82, 256–57, 277–79, 472–74. See also Henry R. Van Til, *The Calvinistic Concept of Culture* (Philadelphia: Presbyterian & Reformed, 2001).

3. Gunton, *Doctrine of Creation*, 1.

4. Obviously, history is most often understood in reference to the past, but note Dale Irvin's comment: "To perceive history as the medium in which we presently live, the water in which we swim, means history is not simply that which is past. History is, of course, that which is past, but it is the past we are in, the past made present as the medium in which we live" (*Christian Histories, Christian Traditioning: Rendering Accounts* [Maryknoll, N.Y.: Orbis, 1998], 18).

5. Another way to put it is to say that the reference to history leads to a focus on human agency in the created order as distinct from theological discussion of the origins of the universe.

is the link: By virtue of the Spirit's preserving activity in creation, history becomes possible and hence the opportunity to steward the created order by means such as cultural development and political involvement. While these may not entail the literal tilling of the soil of creation (though they do involve alteration of creation as given), they are means whereby life within the biophysical order can flourish with the aid of stewardly human action. Moreover, when one understands creation as the biophysical order, the created order is considered to be something that was conceived with development in mind.[6] In other words, the cultural (or dominion) mandate reflects an implicit understanding that the entire biophysical order was created in a state of potential, ready for the long process of development.[7] This development includes the advancement of the human race as well as the flourishing of the environment. Indeed, these imply and demand each other.

The development of humanity is manifested in cultural expression, political involvement, and social order generally. Ordinarily, these three human activities are perceived as historical phenomena that are not normally considered along with the doctrine of creation, yet they can be understood in connection with the created order if human activity on creation's horizon is seen as an implicit responsibility to the creation defined as the biophysical order. The relationship between history and creation's latent potencies, both dependent on the Spirit of God and serving the purposes of God, is the avenue for public theology as expressed here.

Another significant question regarding this definition of creation is, What about the doctrine of the fall? According to this doctrine, the cultural/dominion mandate was given prior to the advent of sin in Eden, yet there is no biblical evidence that the fall voided this mandate. Further, the Noahic covenant, particularly Genesis 9:1–3, reestablished this mandate following the flood narrative. One can only speculate how the mandate would be interpreted apart from a

6. Note Clark Pinnock on this point: "The term *creation* is firmly and mistakenly fixed in people's minds as referring to the initial creative event, not to subsequent history and developments. People too often have the impression that God created the world and then let it run more or less on its own, as though God was active in the world's beginning but not subsequently. As a result the action of the Spirit in natural history is eclipsed" (*Flame of Love: A Theology of the Holy Spirit* [Downers Grove, Ill.: InterVarsity, 1997], 67–68).

7. See n. 2 above.

doctrine of the fall, and we are left to assume that post-fall obedience to the mandate reflects a toil similar to humanity's cursed task in Genesis 3:17–19. There will be fruit, but only by the exertion and toil of much labor, only by painful labor similar to childbirth. The development of the potencies of creation, the slow process of historical advancement, is possible, but it is an arduous task.

Here we need to make a qualification: Terms such as *development* and *advancement* currently have negative connotations in some circles. The implication is that these terms reflect and promote hierarchical and oppressive approaches to interaction with marginalized groups and the planet. Such concerns are valid based on the use of these terms by some people and institutions, but the implication is unwarranted here. While this book contains a view toward positive developments in society, "development" and "advancement" are not indicative of a new colonialist agenda or the worst forms of unbridled capitalist expansion or ecological devastation.

COSMIC PNEUMATOLOGY

The doctrine of the Holy Spirit is often neglected in comparison to the doctrine of God or Christology, and reflection on the cosmic aspect of the Spirit occurs even less frequently,[8] though texts such as Genesis 1:2; Job 27:3; 33:4; 34:14–15; and Psalms 33:6; 104:29–30 speak of this facet of the Spirit's work. Hendrikus Berkhof pointed to this problem in 1964,[9] and apparently there has been little progress since then. As recently as 1997, Clark Pinnock saw the neglect of the Spirit's cosmic activity as directly related to the tendency to focus exclusively on the Spirit's redemptive role:

> So much more attention has been given to the Spirit's work in redemption than the Spirit's work in creation. In Lederle's words, we have made

8. The reality of neglect does not mean that there has been no significant theological reflection on cosmic pneumatology, as an examination of Eastern Orthodoxy, Pietism, or the work of Johann and Christoph Blumhardt reveals. The cosmic aspect of pneumatology is rarely developed in monographs on pneumatology, even if it is mentioned (it may receive a chapter, but even in that case it is rarely of great length), as a survey of volumes on pneumatology shows. There are exceptions, but set against all the volumes written on the Holy Spirit, this kind of neglect is evident.

9. Hendrikus Berkhof, *The Doctrine of the Holy Spirit* (Richmond: John Knox, 1964).

the Spirit into "an ornament of piety." We have read the Bible for its spiritual truth and neglected the material dimensions of its message. We have not emphasized that the Spirit who gives us life in Christ Jesus first gave life to our mortal bodies. Neglect of the cosmic dimension does harm. It minimizes the divine indwelling of the whole world, it reduces salvation to half size by attending to disembodied souls, it fosters forgetfulness about God's concern for ecology, etc. Neglect of the cosmic functions of the Spirit has consequences—let us recover them.[10]

To reflect adequately on the Spirit's cosmic work, it is necessary to reflect on and encourage approaches to pneumatology that bring to light the fullness of the Spirit's work. One way to do this is to counteract the tendency to subsume pneumatology under Christology. This would yield a pneumatology focused directly on the Spirit's distinctive work in the mission of the Trinity and thus in the fullest sense "pneumatic." John McIntyre, reflecting on the problem of pneumatology in relation to Chalcedonian Christology, states the point with great clarity:

> Mention of the christological definition leads us at once to the problem it created for a comparable Spirit definition, namely, the compulsion, as it seemed, to draw up the doctrine of the Spirit on a pattern similar to the style of christology, and to regard the doctrine of the person of Jesus as the evidence for the doctrine of the Spirit. Even though the two doctrines were undeniably connected, as we shall be observing, yet a method which construed the one solely in terms of the other prevented the emergence of the study of the specifically pneumatic character of the doctrine. Nor is it self-evident that the doctrine of the Holy Spirit should be treated as if the Spirit were a further incarnation, an *alter Christus*. In fact, reflection brings out not a few respects in which they are so very different: the Holy Spirit cannot "be seen and heard, touched and handled" as Jesus was; he performs a different role in the *ordo salutis*, the order of salvation, from Jesus; while his relation to human beings would seem to be different from that of Jesus Christ, risen, ascended and glorified. Consequently, we might incline to the conclusion that the application to pneumatology of a method strictly analogical to that followed in christology would lead to the obscuring or even distorting of some of the essential characteristics of the former.[11]

10. Clark Pinnock, "The Role of the Spirit in Creation," *Asbury Theological Journal* 52 (Spring 1997): 49.

11. John McIntyre, *The Shape of Pneumatology: Studies in the Doctrine of the Holy Spirit* (Edinburgh: T & T Clark, 1997), 18–19.

The truly pneumatic character of pneumatology cannot be reached with any clarity if pneumatology is set forth only in a christological paradigm. This leads to the following implication for the Spirit's work in creation: To articulate coherently the cosmic work of the Spirit, we must search for a way to express this pneumatological function according to a pneumatic paradigm. This means the development of a pneumatological logic that complements christological logic.[12] At this point, it should be noted that this call for a pneumatic approach does not carry with it the suggestion that pneumatology should be somehow severed from Christology or that pneumatology should be developed without reference to the Trinity. On the contrary, the proposal to develop a truly pneumatic doctrine of the Spirit with a pneumatological logic is based on the hope of achieving greater clarity regarding the Spirit's work in relation to the Trinity. The Spirit's equality within the Godhead, however, must be taken seriously.

As stated above, cosmic pneumatology deals with the Spirit's work in the biophysical universe. This work of the Spirit is a providential, preserving, indwelling, and life-giving interaction with the created order. It extends back to the beginning of creation but continues into the present and invites us to shape the world toward the future. A primary objective of this book is to achieve a coherent articulation of the function and implications of this aspect of pneumatology. As

12. Arnold A. Van Ruler makes this suggestion in *Calvinist Trinitarianism and Theocentric Politics: Essays toward a Public Theology,* trans. John Bolt (Lewiston, N.Y.: Edwin Mellen, 1989). For a summary of Van Ruler's pneumatological logic, see John Bolt, "The Ecumenical Shift to Cosmic Pneumatology," *Reformed Review* 51 (Spring 98): 255–70. As expressed in the title of his book, McIntyre has a similar pursuit: "When, however, we speak of a 'shape' that is discernible in pneumatology, we have to indicate what is being implied. It is not being suggested that it is a programme followed uniformly by all of the writers dealing with the subject. On the contrary, we shall encounter an immense variety of ways of representing and of addressing the Holy Spirit, some of which are adopted by writers of different persuasions and others selectively employed by the same writer at different times in his or her writing. In looking for 'the shape of pneumatology' we are looking for the components of this rich variety. . . . In a sense, then, we shall be engaged in the first instance in an exercise of taxonomy, a process of classification. Only then will we be better able to move on to the second part of our examination, when we should perhaps change the basic metaphor from the rather static 'taxonomy' to the more dynamic 'anatomy,' for we shall be considering how the various components of the shape thus classified and analysed are fleshed out to operate in relation to one another within the living reality of the Church and the world" (McIntyre, *Shape of Pneumatology,* 21–22).

suggested above, the aim is to express this in a pneumatic fashion according to a pneumatological logic.

PUBLIC THEOLOGY

The relationship between cosmic pneumatology and rigorous, active involvement in the public sphere, ranging from politics to education to science to art, can be understood as public theology. Specifically, public theology in this sense is not only a theological articulation of the rationale for such public engagement or an attempt to argue that religious convictions play a role in the structure and function of society but also a claim that some theological matters are at least comprehensible and at most necessary in public discourse among believers and nonbelievers alike. By showing that the Spirit's cosmic work manifests itself with regard to common grace, this book argues that Kuyper's theology of culture and politics is ultimately rooted in such a pneumatology. Kuyper's work demonstrates the connection between cosmic pneumatology and public engagement, particularly the Spirit's enablement to utilize and manage the resources of creation in a stewardly fashion, and provides a frame of reference for further theological reflection on this aspect of the Spirit's work. The next introductory step is to weave together the strands of cosmic pneumatology, public theology, and Kuyper's life into a thread that prepares the way for the remaining chapters of this book.

CONTEMPORARY COSMIC PNEUMATOLOGY

Recent decades have seen a resurgence of reflection on the doctrine of the Holy Spirit. Some of these authors significantly address the Spirit's role in creation. A summary of the work of six authors on this issue provides the first strand of the thread. Mapping the contemporary terrain of systematic theological reflection on cosmic pneumatology raises the pertinent questions that will bring this study into greater focus.

Geiko Müller-Fahrenholz

As revealed in its subtitle, *God's Spirit: Transforming a World in Crisis* focuses on global concerns (e.g., nuclear threats, poverty, and environmental hazards). Most pertinent to contemporary cosmic pneumatology is the first part of the book, titled "Creator Spirit—Soul of the World." In part 1, four ideas are expressed that directly contribute to cosmic pneumatology.

First, Geiko Müller-Fahrenholz argues that the invocation of God's Spirit yields a perspective on the world in which it "becomes 'creation,' and thus acquires an axiomatic and essential dignity and value."[13] For Müller-Fahrenholz, "creation" is a mythic category that is not merely synonymous with terms such as *nature* and *universe*. The mythic status of creation "preserves the inviolable subjectivity of all things, their ineradicably unique value and primordial status."[14] The use of this category provides a kind of protection for creation and creates the opportunity for discourse that may lead to solutions to various global crises.

Second, Müller-Fahrenholz refers to the Holy Spirit as the basic principle of creation. The divine *rûaḥ* (Spirit) is present when God speaks at the inception of creation, a form of speaking that includes action and process. The Spirit creates the space for life to unfold. Regarding the Trinity, Müller-Fahrenholz takes a perichoretic perspective, which enables divine speech to be seen as a dialogical process of response, communication, and exchange. As a process, divine breathing leads to increasingly complex forms of life, hence continued differentiation, which logically leads to the final creation of humanity.[15]

In addition to discussing the function of the divine *rûaḥ*, Müller-Fahrenholz suggests the following analogy between the inception of creation and pregnancy:

A pregnant woman prepares *within herself* the space for a living creature that is not herself yet draws its life from her. In this sense, it would be more logical to conceive of the "primeval space" of creation as a mother's womb. . . . Is there any reason to reject the idea of creation as a bringing forth for which the most appropriate analogy is that of the process of gestation within and delivery by a mother? Why should we not express the inexpressible concept of creation by recourse to the image of pregnancy? . . . Why should we not think of the primeval

13. Geiko Müller-Fahrenholz, *God's Spirit: Transforming a World in Crisis* (Geneva: WCC Publications, 1995), 8.
14. Ibid.
15. Ibid., 14.

space of creation as the process of gestation, in the sense that what
we will eventually be has not yet emerged?[16]

While it refers to process, the metaphor used in this analogy also
refers to mercy and intimacy, a connection made evident by the
fact that Hebrew uses the same word for "womb" and "mercy."
Müller-Fahrenholz admits that the specter of pantheism looms
quite large but responds that this metaphor is only one way of
emphasizing the divine origin of creation, in a manner similar to
Psalm 33:6 and Psalm 104, among other biblical passages. He
further admits that a disadvantage of the pregnancy image is that
pregnancy has a definite chronological conclusion and is not an
end in itself (it leads to an independent life form that continually
moves farther away from the maternal presence), whereas creation
and eschatological fulfillment maintain a constant, dependent relationship with God. Rather than abandoning the image however,
we are called to recognize the limits of the metaphor. The purpose
of this metaphor is

> to illuminate the intimacy and selflessness of God's concentration on all
> creation, and to clarify the function of the space and time of creation
> within God's space-time. The same metaphor can also help correct
> the unilaterally male tendency in our image of God, by allowing us
> to understand God's power as the omnipotence of love and not as the
> overbearing might of a potentate.[17]

Third is a vision of fertility. The acknowledgment of the Creator
Spirit yields a recognition of the fruitfulness of all life, an original
blessing of fertility at creation. This blessing also includes the dominion mandate. Müller-Fahrenholz perceives this as "shaping" the
world and views cultural development as an artificial adaptation to
natural life conditions.[18] The development of culture is currently in
crisis because both procreation and consumption have become destructive. In Müller-Fahrenholz's view, "Procreation without order
and consumption without reconstruction are both forms of uncon-
trolled 'fertility' that betray the commission to cultivate and preserve.
They do not fill the earth but empty it. They do not shape the fabric

16. Ibid., 15.
17. Ibid., 17.
18. Ibid., 23.

of life but tear deep holes in it."[19] In spite of this, the hopeful vision is that fertility and creativity can be perceived as shaping forces by large numbers of people and that "self-preservation will become a function of self-control."[20]

Last is a view of the Spirit's sustaining work. "The motherly *rûach* sustains all created things with its loving energy and thus unites the work of creation and the work of redemption."[21] As expressed in Psalm 104, the Spirit is "the inexhaustible power which as the soul of the world bestows breath and order, energy and love of life on all things. It is the divine power that maintains creation . . . the power that prompts creation onwards because it has not yet reached its goal."[22] The divine spiration is like a kiss of life and a form of mouth-to-mouth resuscitation (e.g., Gen. 2:7 shows intimacy between Creator and creature as Adam is given the breath of life). This metaphor reveals the closeness between God and creation and also emphasizes creation as continuous.[23]

Müller-Fahrenholz presents an approach to cosmic pneumatology that strives to engender a more peaceful society. His four ideas raise the question of the relationship between pneumatology and human responsibility in the world. Through categories such as fertility and the womb metaphor, we are prompted to ask whether the Spirit's cosmic work promotes particular approaches to ecology and cultural development. In addition, the pantheistic tendencies in this work prompt the question of the proximity of the identities of God and creation. Does the Spirit's presence in creation require the use of metaphors or analogies that seem to make God a part of the world?

Sinclair Ferguson

Two sections of *The Holy Spirit* address cosmic pneumatology. In the first chapter, "The Holy Spirit and His Story," Sinclair Ferguson describes the divine *rûah* as "the irresistible force, the all-powerful energy of God in the created order. He cannot be 'tamed' by men.

---

19. Ibid., 24.
20. Ibid.
21. Ibid., 27.
22. Ibid.
23. Müller-Fahrenholz proposes a concept called *ecodomy* (chap. 18 is titled "Ecodomy—Building the House of Life"), in which churches seek to preserve and restore the world. This involves such things as the eradication of poverty, population control, a matriarchal shift, and the strengthening of civil society (ibid., chaps. 18–23).

Instead, through his *ruach* he is able to 'tame' or subdue all things to fulfill his own purpose."[24] More than simply the divine energy, *rûaḥ* describes God's personal extension toward and active engagement with the creation.

More specifically, according to Ferguson's interpretation of Genesis 1:2, the Spirit's hovering presence establishes cosmic order.[25] The activity of God in creation extends the divine presence into the world for the purpose of ordering and completing what has been planned in the mind of God.[26] Ferguson notices a complementarity between the language of the divine *rûaḥ* and the face of God (as in Ps. 104:29), as both indicate personal divine presence. At the close of the section, Ferguson refers to the Spirit's presence as the "executive" in ordering and governing the created order.

Ferguson's final chapter is titled "The Cosmic Spirit" and broadly addresses the Spirit's role in creation and redemption. Though he finds that the New Testament reveals an antithetical Spirit/world relationship, he argues that the Spirit's executive role in creation provides the diverse capacities and abilities present in the human race. In Ferguson's view:

> [The Spirit] is the minister of the kindness of God in relation to the just and the unjust alike (Mt. 5:45). But these are exhibitions of God's restraining mercy while his Spirit contends with man (Gn. 6:3). Without this the world would either destroy itself or be destroyed. The mercy is real, but it is not arbitrary. It is set within limits and has a view to repentance (Rom. 2:4; 2 Pet. 3:3–9). It is within this context alone that this general ministry of the Spirit should be assessed. All the more so because it is clear in the New Testament that even the exercise of

24. Sinclair Ferguson, *The Holy Spirit* (Downers Grove, Ill.: InterVarsity, 1996), 18. For purposes of convenience, Ferguson transliterates (רוח) as *ruach* instead of the more technically correct *rûaḥ*.

25. Ibid., 19. Ferguson also makes the following interesting observation: "Indeed, while generally unnoticed in the exposition in Genesis 1, it can be argued that recognizing the presence of the divine Spirit in Genesis 1:2 would provide the 'missing link' in interpretation of the 'Let *us* make . . .' in Genesis 1:26–27. The Spirit of God would then be the only possible referent of this address *within the structure of the account itself.* In this case, the engagement of the Spirit in the work of creation would mark the beginning and end of a literary *inclusio* in Genesis 1" (ibid., 20–21).

26. Ibid., 21. It is important to mention that Ferguson constructs this section around a discussion of whether the Genesis narrative can be understood as making reference to the members of the Trinity. Thus, the argument articulates the Spirit's identity and work in reference to exegetical discussion of the meaning of *rûaḥ*.

"spiritual gifts" should never be identified with the Spirit's work in saving grace. It is possible for the former to be present where the latter is, sadly, absent.[27]

In agreement with Calvin, Ferguson views the various human talents and capacities as general gifts of the Spirit that are nonsalvific.[28]

Ferguson's use of the term *executive* to describe the Spirit's work in creation and his argument that the Spirit established cosmic order at the beginning of creation lead to questions that are directly pertinent to public theology and to the significance of the Spirit's role in common grace. If the Spirit is perceived to be the member of the Trinity who carries out divine directives, it is important to inquire about the manner in which such an agency relates to the roles of the other members of the Godhead in their interaction with creation. Furthermore, the establishment of order leads to an inquiry concerning the structure of not only creation but also the society that emerges as humans carry out the directive that Reformed theology calls the cultural mandate. Does the cosmic activity of the Spirit merit distinction by virtue of an executive role, and does the Spirit really provide a means toward anything other than a general management of creation? Could there be implications for culture and politics?

Colin Gunton

Christ and Creation, a published version of the Didsbury Lectures, presents insights on the relationship between the Spirit and creation in lectures three and four. The third, "Incarnation, Kenosis, and Divine Action," speaks of the Spirit in the context of a trinitarian understanding of creation. First, the fact that creation is christological as well as pneumatological reveals that creation has a teleology, a specific direction. The end of this teleology is that creation will ultimately praise its Creator and return to its Maker.[29] Against a general pantheist and panentheist understanding of the God/world relation, Colin Gunton views the divine activity in the world as particular and enabling. The world possesses its distinctive being by the Spirit's power, and this

27. Ibid., 247.
28. Ibid., 248. Ferguson says little about any sociopolitical implications of the Spirit's cosmic work and instead focuses primarily on the Spirit's re-creative role in the eschaton, from transformation of humans to the larger transformation of the created order.
29. Colin E. Gunton, *Christ and Creation* (Grand Rapids: Eerdmans, 1992), 77.

empowerment enables creation to be itself rather than a tool or an extension of God, especially in view of its teleology. Creation is free to move toward perfection by the Spirit's direction.

The fourth lecture, "In the Image and Likeness of God," includes reflections on the implications of the Spirit's role in creation. Gunton first expresses the Spirit's role in divine imaging as the realization of a particular pattern of life on earth (primarily through the renewal of the image in Christians), the *telos* of which is to enable creation to reach its perfection.[30] The final section speaks of a transformative role of the Spirit that includes ecological implications. Hardly a triumphalist on such matters, Gunton argues that "the distinctively Christian contributions to the process are in generating an awareness of the penultimacy of all matters to do with this world of time and space, and yet of the capacity that even this penultimate has to praise the God who made it."[31] While humans cannot perfect creation, they can enable the praise of creation through the Spirit's impulse. Gunton's emphasis on teleology raises a significant question for this book: Does a *telos* of praise and a return to the Creator lead to a neglect of Spirit-prompted engagement in the world? This is made all the more interesting by Gunton's point that matters of this world are penultimate. Penultimacy, in spite of Gunton's recognition of the importance of leading creation toward the praise of God in this life, can have the unintended effect of rendering cultural and political engagement insignificant. While Gunton would like to encourage Christian action that enables the praise of creation as it moves toward perfection, do his emphases, in some sense, actually impede our participation in this process?

Jürgen Moltmann

While Jürgen Moltmann has written three books that mention cosmic pneumatology, *God in Creation* most thoroughly covers

30. Ibid., 103.

31. Ibid., 124. Gunton also includes art as a way that the Spirit leads creation to its *telos*. From another angle, he criticizes the industrialized approach to meat production as offensive to the goodness of the Creator, though he hesitates to condemn the eating of animals. In terms of perspective, it is important to note that Gunton does perceive pneumatological transformation through a christological lens: "The Spirit transforms only in relation to the work of the crucified" (see ibid., 123–24). Gunton's approach to cosmic pneumatology is also covered in Colin Gunton, *The Triune Creator: A Historical and Systematic Study* (Edinburgh: Edinburgh University Press, 1998).

this aspect of the Holy Spirit's work.[32] The central concern of the book is to articulate a doctrine of creation that counteracts the human technological exploitation of the world and "to discover God *in* all the beings he has created and to find his life-giving Spirit *in* the community of creation that they share."[33] From the outset, Moltmann acknowledges that his view of Spirit/creation relationship is panentheistic, which requires us to "bring reverence for the life of every living thing into the adoration of God."[34] The practical objective is to expand service of God into service for the creation.

Chapters 1 and 4 bring Moltmann's cosmic pneumatology into focus. The fifth section of chapter 1, "Creation in the Spirit," approaches the trinitarian understanding of creation from a pneumatological perspective. Drawing on Psalm 104, Moltmann articulates the Spirit's relationship to creation:

> It is always the Spirit who first brings the activity of the Father and Son to its goal. It follows that the triune God also unremittingly breathes the Spirit into his creation. Everything that is, exists and lives in the unceasing flow of the energies and potentialities of the cosmic Spirit. This means that we have to understand every created reality in terms of energy, grasping it as the realized potentiality of the divine Spirit. Through the energies and potentialities of the Spirit, the Creator is himself present in his creation. He does not merely confront it in his transcendence; entering into it, he is also immanent in it.[35]

The immanence of the Spirit in creation leads to the assumption that this Spirit is poured out on all that exists and that the divine Spirit preserves, animates, and renews the created order.

Acknowledging Calvin's contribution to the concept of creation in the Spirit,[36] Moltmann moves from a recognition of the Spirit as the

32. *Spirit of Life* and *Source of Life* (see n. 1 above) rehearse the insights of *God in Creation* but do not advance beyond them. In the two former books, Moltmann has different agendas. *Spirit of Life* is focused more on Christian life and the Trinity, and *Source of Life* is a volume for practical theology.

33. Moltmann, *God in Creation*, xi.

34. Ibid., xii.

35. Ibid., 9.

36. Moltmann's perception is that Calvin "was one of the few people to take up and maintain this conception" (ibid., 11). Elsewhere he expresses the following opinion regarding the reluctance to reflect on the Spirit's cosmic work: "One reason is certainly

"fountain of life" to the idea that the Spirit's universal outpouring creates a community of created things with God and one another. This means that "everything exists, lives, and moves *in others,* in one another, with one another, for one another, in the cosmic interrelations of the divine Spirit."[37] The implication is that coactivity is part of creation's essential being. There is no such thing as a solitary life. For Moltmann, this kind of interrelation is modeled by the Trinity in the concept of *perichōrēsis.*[38] This approach is not pantheistic, because God's action and penetration into creation occur without him becoming merged with it. "The cosmic Spirit remains God's Spirit, and becomes our Spirit since he acts in us as the power that makes us live."[39] The result of this view regarding creation and pneumatology is an approach to the earth that moves beyond the age of subjectivity and mechanistic world domination to hope for a "peaceful, ecological world-wide community in solidarity."[40]

The fifth section of chapter 4 is titled "The Cosmic Spirit." In response to the mechanistic worldview, which made the world calculable and open to human subjection, Moltmann articulates a view of creation rooted in pneumatology. From this perspective, the world is a "fabric woven by the Spirit, and is therefore a reality to which the Spirit gives form."[41]

How does the cosmic Spirit operate in nature? Moltmann presents the following four ways:

1. The Spirit is the principle of creativity, creating new possibilities and anticipating the new designs and blueprints for material and living organisms.

---

the continuing Platonization of Christianity. Even today this still puts its mark on what is termed 'spirituality' in the church and religious groups. It takes the form of a kind of hostility to the body, a kind of remoteness from the world, and a preference for the inner experiences of the soul rather than the sensory experiences of sociality and nature. Another reason, I believe, is the far-reaching decision in favor of the *filioque.* This has meant that the Holy Spirit has come to be understood solely as 'the Spirit of Christ,' and not at the same time as 'the Spirit of the Father.' . . . If redemption is placed in radical discontinuity to creation then 'the Spirit of Christ' has no longer anything to do with Yahweh's *ruach*" (Moltmann, *Spirit of Life,* 8–9).

37. Moltmann, *God in Creation,* 11.
38. Ibid., 16–17.
39. Ibid., 12.
40. Ibid., 13.
41. Ibid., 99.

2. The Spirit is the holistic principle, leading to mutual *perichōrēsis* and therefore a life of cooperation and community. The Holy Spirit is the "common Spirit" of creation.
3. The Spirit is also the principle of individuation, differentiating particular "working sketches" of matter and life on their various levels. Self-assertion and integration, self-preservation and self-transcendence are the two complementary sides of the process through which life evolves.
4. All creations of the Spirit are "open" in intention, directed toward their common future, because they are all aligned toward their potentialities. The principle of intentionality is inherent in all open systems of matter and life.[42]

The Spirit's pervasive operation in the world means that each individual is seen as part of the whole. The created order consists of individuations of the community of creation and manifestations of the Spirit. The Spirit's presence in all creation imbues it with self-transcendence, which is the only way to conceive of the presence of the infinite in the finite without the infinite destroying the finite or vice versa.

Drawing on Romans 8:19–22, which speaks of creation's groaning for redemption, Moltmann perceives a solidarity between believers and other created things:

> So what believers experience and perceive in the Holy Spirit reveals the structure of the Spirit of creation, the human spirit, and the Spirit in the whole of non-human creation; because it is to this that their experience corresponds. What believers experience in the Holy Spirit leads them into solidarity with all other created things. They suffer *with* nature under the power of transience, and they hope *for* nature, waiting for the manifestation of liberty.[43]

As creation endures its suffering history, the indwelling Spirit turns that history into a history of hope. "The presence of the Spirit of creation generates the hope of created things in the difference between life and suffering."[44]

How does Moltmann view the question of panentheism? For him, the difference between pantheism and panentheism is that the for-

42. Ibid., 100.
43. Ibid., 101.
44. Ibid., 102.

mer sees merely divine presence whereas the latter is able to discern future transcendence, evolution, and intentionality.[45] In addition to a panentheist concept of the Spirit-earth relation, Moltmann utilizes trinitarian doctrine to express the fact of divine transcendence and immanence. The trinitarian doctrine conceives of creation as an interconnected web of processes. In this, the Spirit both binds together and differentiates as well as preserves and leads living things and their communities beyond themselves. The indwelling Spirit is fundamental to the community of creation, and in contrast to the mechanistic worldview (which sees elementary particles as basic to more complex entities), the world's complex harmony of relations and self-transcending movements are basic. In this complexity, the Spirit's longing for a still unattained consummation finds expression. Since the cosmic Spirit is the divine Spirit, Moltmann concludes that the universe cannot be viewed as a closed system but one that is open for God and his future. This means there is hope for creation and also that creation will be respected instead of dominated.

Moltmann's explicit panentheism raises the question of whether there is a way to articulate the divine presence on the earth while maintaining divine transcendence. Is panentheism an adequate category? Moltmann's concerns about a mechanistic approach to the world make him cautious of dominion language. Is it necessary to find alternative language for the approach to the world prompted by cosmic pneumatology? In addition, what is the proper approach to technology and development in view of the negative consequences yielded by the mechanistic worldview? Finally, what is the extent of the hope provided by Moltmann's understanding of Romans 8 and his open view of the future? What is the appropriate level of optimism for Spirit-prompted public engagement?

Clark Pinnock

The second chapter of *Flame of Love* is dedicated to the Holy Spirit in creation. Clark Pinnock writes of the Spirit as life-giver, with a central role at creation's inception. He also refers to the Spirit as "the ecstasy that implements God's abundance and triggers the overflow of divine self-giving."[46] This leads him to view the Spirit as the power of creation and to a recognition of the Spirit's activity in the world

45. Ibid., 103.
46. Pinnock, *Flame of Love,* 50.

and history, particularly in terms of development and consummation. The entire universe is the domain of the Spirit's operations. Pinnock expresses the significance of cosmic pneumatology in this way:

> The Spirit as life-giver and universal divine presence, while not an oft-repeated theme, is nonetheless a weighty concept in the Bible. God is not just *before* creation as its initiator but also *with* creation in its development as its director. Spirit is the ground of the world's becoming and brings God into an intimate relationship with the world. Spirit introduces love into the world, sustains life and gives meaning. The Spirit is with humanity on its journey through time and with the creation in its groaning and longing for deliverance. We are surrounded by the mystery of God, "in [whom] we live and move and have our being (Acts 17:8)."[47]

Pinnock begins his reflection by clarifying the Spirit/creation relationship. Making reference to biblical texts found in Genesis, Job, Psalms, Proverbs, and Acts,[48] he establishes the Spirit's role as giver, sustainer, and perfecter of life and creation. In addition, he points to the link between the Spirit and wisdom, noting how both are portrayed as the agent of divine creativity. This leads to a view of the God/creation relationship that allows us to recognize the divine presence throughout creation. It also reveals the cosmic pneumatological aspect of the doctrine of providence, which at least indirectly refers to the Spirit's moving in the continuing creation. Pinnock speaks of it this way: "The Spirit has been implementing God's purposes for creation from day one and is committed to seeing to it that they issue in restoration. Creator Spirit inspires hope for a world beyond the reach of humanity, in which God's power raises the dead and makes everything new."[49]

47. Ibid., 51.
48. Regarding the few texts that speak of this aspect, Pinnock says, "The relative scarcity of such texts does not make the truth unimportant. Creation as a doctrine generally tends to be taken for granted and is treated infrequently and cursorily in biblical study. Even the 'creation out of nothing' that theologians consider important goes unmentioned in the Bible. It is deduced from other verses. But the importance of a truth cannot be measured by counting verses. The fact is that the doctrine of creation and the Spirit's role in it is supported both by scriptural texts and by theological reflection on them. Scripture makes it clear enough that God created all things and that the Spirit is present everywhere in the world. The point does not have to be repeated often to hold true" (ibid., 52–53).
49. Ibid., 54.

Reflecting on the neglect of the cosmic and creational role of the Spirit, Pinnock points to the negative consequences of such disregard.[50] The major consequence is the separation of creation and redemption into spheres with a line drawn between them. The result is that creation is downgraded to an event preparatory to redemption. Pinnock does acknowledge that theologians such as Calvin and Kuyper reflected on the Spirit's cosmic dimensions, and he calls for a courageous pneumatology that includes the cosmic element in spite of fears of speculative abuse.

Reflecting on creation from a trinitarian perspective, Pinnock articulates a relational view of the Trinity in which the loving relationships of Father, Son, and Spirit yield creative activity. Creation is an act of God's pleasure and exists in a kind of relative autonomy. Pinnock perceives creation as distinct from God, and he views history as neither random nor predetermined but a theater in which the Spirit choreographs "the dance of creation by analogy to what he does in the fellowship of the sublime Trinity."[51] Considered the bond of love who fosters fellowship, the Spirit makes possible the relationship between God and the world. Teleologically, the Spirit moves creation toward perfection by bringing into being increasingly complex entities, hence moving the world toward a greater display of the divine likeness in history.

Speaking more directly about the Spirit's trinitarian role in creation, Pinnock notes that while creation is created by God through the Son, it is also a result of the breathing of the Spirit. The divine breath mediates the divine presence in creation and enables union between the creature and God. Picturing the Trinity as a spiral action that releases the power of its momentum outwardly, Pinnock says that the Spirit "seeks to reproduce in the world the interior mystery of God, ever spiraling it back toward God."[52] In comparison to the Son as ordering *Logos,* the Spirit is the artisan who ensures the advent, development, and fulfillment of creaturely forms. As in Genesis 1:2,

---

50. Using W. H. Griffith Thomas as an example, Pinnock also points to concerns raised by reflection on the Spirit's work on a universal scale. These fears concern theological revisionism based on questions such as, "What if people thought they detected the stirrings of the Spirit in the heathen world? What if the uniqueness of Jesus Christ were diminished as too much thought was given to the Spirit's global presence?" (ibid., 54).

51. Ibid., 56.

52. Ibid., 60.

the Spirit leads creation toward a goal of sabbath rest (new creation) by continuing to energize and sustain the world throughout history. Significantly, Pinnock points to the following implication of the Spirit's cosmic work: "As the power of creation, the Spirit *does not call us to escape from the world or from history*, but keeps creation open to the future."[53]

Pinnock articulates three additional implications of the Spirit's role in creation.[54] The first is that the recognition of God's involvement in the fullness of creation reveals a created order that can be perceived as a natural sacrament. All of creation is graced by the Spirit's presence. Second, the link between creation and redemption is kept open by acknowledgment of the Creator Spirit. "Spirit is the power of redemption only because he is first the power of creation. Only the Spirit of creation is strong enough to be the Spirit of resurrection."[55] For Pinnock, the Creator Spirit's global activity is also a source of hope that no one is beyond the reach of grace. Last, the Spirit's role in creation encourages ecological responsibility and stewardship of the earth.[56]

Pinnock's work, while highlighting the previously mentioned issues of the relationship of the Spirit within the Trinity, teleology, and cosmic order, raises the issue of public engagement in a helpful way by specifically noting the Spirit's impulse toward engagement in the world and history. While he does not offer cultural or sociopolitical suggestions, he renders the possibility of public activity by more directly linking teleology to responsibility in this present age. Similar to Moltmann and Müller-Fahrenholz, he echoes concern for the care of creation.

Finally, Pinnock touches on the relationship between creation and redemption. His desire to erase the line between God's work in creation and his work in redemption prompts the inquiry regarding the best way to articulate their relationship. How does one arrive at an appropriate emphasis on the Spirit and creation while also speaking of redemption? The work of the Spirit in creation requires distinc-

---

53. Ibid., 61.
54. He also addresses the issues of science and origins in this chapter, but they are not directly relevant.
55. Pinnock, *Flame of Love*, 63.
56. Pinnock says a little more about ecological responsibility at the end of the chapter, but he does not strongly emphasize responsibility for stewarding creation. It is more implication than anything else.

tion, but how is this done without hinting at a relatively independent pneumatology?

Mark Wallace

The introduction of the postmodern and ecologically minded *Fragments of the Spirit: Nature, Violence, and the Renewal of Creation* defines the Spirit as "the power of life giving breath (*rûah*) within the cosmos who continually works to transform and renew all forms of life—both human and nonhuman."[57] Mark Wallace seeks to present the Holy Spirit as "God's invigorating presence within the society of all living beings. This life-centered model of the Spirit expands beyond an *intratrinitarian* role (traditionally expressed as the bond of unity between the Father and the Son) to include the Spirit's *cosmic* role as the power of healing and renewal within all creation."[58] This cosmic pneumatology is expressed most explicitly in the fifth chapter, "The Spirit and Nature: The Wild Bird Who Heals," which is designed to move toward a biocentric, ecological pneumatology.

The first section of this chapter rehearses threats to the environment (e.g., acid rain, ozone depletion, pesticides, radioactive waste, and overpopulation) that Wallace calls "the specter of ecocide." His response lies in the recovery of a pneumatology that views the Holy Spirit as a "natural, living being who indwells and sustains all life-forms."[59] In this approach, a key aspect of the Spirit's task is to lead creation toward a peaceable interrelationship. In terms of the Spirit/earth relationship, Wallace views this interrelationship as a coinherence that maintains differentiation. This coinherence is so close as to make the Spirit and earth inseparable, though there is distinction. The Spirit inhabits the earth as *rûah* (invisible and life-giving breath), and the earth (*gaia*) is the outward manifestation of the Spirit's invisible sustaining presence. With others, such as Pinnock, Wallace perceives that this understanding of the Spirit was not emphasized in the twentieth century.[60] He points to the abundant scriptural imagery (vivifying breath, healing wind,

57. Mark I. Wallace, *Fragments of the Spirit: Nature, Violence, and the Renewal of Creation* (New York: Continuum, 1996), 1.

58. Ibid.

59. Ibid., 136.

60. Ibid., 137. Wallace does acknowledge the work of Moltmann but laments this deemphasis in the works of H. Berkhof (*Theologie des Heiligen Geistes*), Yves Congar (*I Believe in the Holy Spirit*), George S. Hendry (*The Holy Spirit in Christian Theology*), Alisdair I. C. Heron (*The Holy Spirit: The Holy Spirit in the Bible, the History of Chris-*

living water, purgative fire, and divine dove) to validate an emphasis on the Spirit as the Spirit of creation. The reconception of the Spirit as a natural entity does have one large caveat, however:

> One intriguing but troubling implication of an ecological pneumatology of internal relatedness is that it places the divine life at risk in a manner that an extrinsic doctrine of the Spirit vis-à-vis the earth does not. *If the Spirit and earth mutually indwell each other, then God as Spirit is vulnerable to loss and destruction insofar as the earth is abused and despoiled.* While this association is beginning to be felt by many people today, most theologians are hesitant to postulate that ecologically toxic relationships with other life-forms places the presence of the Spirit in the world in fundamental jeopardy.[61]

Wallace advances his biocentric approach in several modes. In conversation with Sallie McFague, Native American spirituality, and neopagan environmentalist activists, he puts forward a revisionary paganism, suggesting that the divine presence in creation indwells all living things. The intent of this approach, which he acknowledges is susceptible to charges of pantheism, is to revision creation as a sacred grove, a living sacrament, instead of a subject of stewardship and domination. Rather than stewardship, Wallace proposes a *friendship* ideal for an environmental ethic.[62] In speaking of the Spirit's relationships within the Trinity and the universe, Wallace articulates the Spirit's identity as the *vinculum caritatis* (bond of love) within the life of God and the life of the cosmos. With reference to creation, the Spirit's ministry is to keep creation alive (*continuata creatio*). This corresponds to the Spirit's role as the promoter of unity, intimacy, and reciprocity in the trinitarian life as well as in human transformation. Wallace perceives the Spirit's promotion of unity as a force in removing artificial boundaries between the human and nonhuman orders, hopefully resulting in compassion for all life-forms.

In a section titled "Composting Religion," Wallace suggests that a resensitization to the Spirit's double identity as personal agent and

---

tian *Thought, and Recent Theology*), G. W. H. Lampe (*God as Spirit*), and John V. Taylor (*The Go-Between God: The Holy Spirit and the Christian Mission*). In spite of this criticism, Wallace does have a high regard for these volumes.

61. Ibid., 138.

62. Ibid., 144. Wallace acknowledges that people may be uncomfortable with his biophilic "Christian paganism" but argues that the current crisis demands such a radical approach.

inanimate force can serve as an index to the common destiny of human and nonhuman creatures. This dual identity implies that every aspect of creation (indwelt by the Spirit) should be understood in personal and impersonal terms. The "personhood" of the nonhuman order has significant implications for the "partnership" of humans and other life-forms in the biotic community.[63]

Wallace draws on the work of John Muir to articulate further the intimacy of Spirit and creation. Noting that Muir espoused a "wilderness" pneumatology that perceived glimpses of the divine presence throughout the natural order, Wallace points to the loss of distinctions "between humankind and otherkind that results from an all-consuming earth love."[64] This kind of biophilia is paradigmatic for Wallace's attempt to develop a life-centered pneumatology for this era. In the Bible, Wallace finds a biocentric perspective in God's response to Job (the divine interrogation reveals to Job that humans are not the center of creation and that Job must resituate himself among the created order), and he views Genesis 1 as "a nonanthropocentric ordering of all life-forms into a cosmic, biocentric harmony that precedes and envelops the salvation-history account of the Yahwist redactors."[65] He interprets the narrative in Genesis 2 as suspending humankind within an interconnected biological web of plants and animals. In all of this, the Spirit animates all life-forms in the same manner. Humans are not privileged over the other species.

Wallace attempts to move beyond the stewardship model of the human/creation relationship by suggesting that humans consider themselves pilgrims who should practice a hands-off ethic toward other life-forms.[66] His ecological pneumatology, which perceives the Spirit as a wild life-form who transgresses the boundaries between human and nonhuman life, "embodies the promise of a new nature-intoxicated spirituality that knocks humankind off its hierarchical pedestal and replants it within the great earth mother, vitalized by the Spirit, who gives life to all beings."[67] Wallace, in the end, hopes

63. Ibid., 154.
64. Ibid., 156.
65. Ibid., 161.
66. Ibid., 167. This is where Wallace differs significantly from Moltmann. While he admires Moltmann's approach, he laments the fact that there is still a distinction made that places humanity above the rest of creation.
67. Ibid., 167–68. Wallace is aware that his approach threatens traditional assumptions and identities, but the eco-crisis drives his approach.

to inspire a kind of eco-solidarity that will lead to the healing and revivification of the earth.[68]

Wallace's work is clearly the most radical of all the authors presented here. It cannot be said that his concerns are not valid. The point of inquiry concerns whether a biophilic, stewardship resistant approach is necessary. Like Moltmann, Wallace articulates a pan-entheistic perspective, though Wallace pushes for an even greater respect for creation. Wallace's work leads to three questions, some similar to those raised by others. What is the wisest approach to the threatened planet? How much does the Spirit's presence in creation curb the "development" of the world? What is the best way to cultivate creation?[69]

The Need for Another Cosmic Pneumatology?

As this survey has shown, there are a variety of methods and emphases in contemporary cosmic pneumatology. Müller-Fahrenholz, Moltmann, and Wallace lean toward pantheistic and panentheistic perspectives of the God/world relationship as a result of the Spirit's immanence in creation, while Ferguson, Gunton, and Pinnock emphasize more traditionally orthodox perspectives. Their various methods emphasize fidelity to themes and sources ranging from biblical to christological to ecological, and all six authors raise significant questions.

Given this range of contributions, the question arises as to how the present work is different. The answer is that these contributions are in some sense inadequate, either because of their conception of cosmic pneumatology or because of a problem with their range of and approach to the implications drawn from the doctrine. As an example, apart from Pinnock, these authors do not address the Spirit's role as it involves creation and history, though they may make reference to nature understood as the biophysical universe (Wallace and Moltmann especially). Furthermore, there is a paucity of reflection on the public implications of the more orthodox pneumatologies, while the more progressive pneumatologies encourage political agendas (e.g.,

---

68. Ibid., 168–70.
69. Wallace is in the process of answering these and other questions in his forthcoming volume *Earth God: A Neopagan Christian Spirituality*. This text will further develop Wallace's cosmic pneumatology as he explores the idea of Christianity as an earth-centered religion.

biophilic and eco-centric) that contrast with the Kuyperian cosmic pneumatology and public theology in this book.

Yet these authors have raised intriguing questions for the further development of this aspect of pneumatological doctrine, particularly in two areas. First, there is the question of the language and categories used to describe the function of the Spirit in creation. How might one articulate the Spirit's nonredemptive work in the created order? Is there a way to do this that is not pantheistic or panentheistic yet yields at least an adequate if not robust respect for the world? How does one speak of the Spirit's work in a manner that is distinctive but appropriately trinitarian? The second area of inquiry follows from this. What approach to public engagement arises from the language and categories chosen to articulate the Spirit's cosmic work? What kind of public theology will be the result? These concerns are addressed in chapter 4, the constructive part of this book.

PUBLIC THEOLOGY

Public theology is the second strand in the thread. Two approaches to public theology are relevant for the purposes of this book. One approach is apologetic, as represented by Max Stackhouse.[70] The second approach is confessional, as represented by Ronald Thiemann.[71]

70. There are other authors who take an apologetic approach, though they differ on many issues. See David Tracy, *The Analogical Imagination: Christian Theology and the Culture of Pluralism* (New York: Crossroad, 1981); Robert Benne, *The Paradoxical Vision: A Public Theology for the Twenty-first Century* (Minneapolis: Fortress, 1995); and Glenn Tinder, *The Political Meaning of Christianity: An Interpretation* (Baton Rouge: Louisiana State University Press, 1989).

71. Among other confessional theologians, most of whom can be loosely identified as "postliberals," see William Placher, *Unapologetic Theology: A Christian Voice in a Pluralistic Conversation* (Louisville: Westminster John Knox, 1989); George Lindbeck, *The Nature of Doctrine: Religion and Theology in a Postliberal Age* (Philadelphia: Westminster, 1984); Stanley Hauerwas, *The Peaceable Kingdom: A Primer in Christian Ethics* (Notre Dame: University of Notre Dame Press, 1983); and John Howard Yoder, *For the Nations: Essays Public and Political* (Grand Rapids: Eerdmans, 1997). Thiemann's work more than adequately sets forth this approach to public theology. He does differ from the others in some ways, particularly Hauerwas and Lindbeck, but they all share certain core similarities.

Max Stackhouse

Stackhouse defines public theology as follows:

> First, . . . that which we as Christians believe we have to offer the world for its salvation is not esoteric, privileged, irrational, or inaccessible. It is something that we believe to be both comprehensible and indispensable for all, something that we can reasonably discuss with Hindus and Buddhists, Jews and Muslims, Humanists and Marxists. Second, such a theology will give guidance to the structures and policies of public life. It is ethical in nature. The truth for which we argue must imply a viable element of justice, and its adequacy can be tested on that basis.[72]

Stackhouse notices a crisis in contemporary society that is in part (if not wholly) rooted in a societal amnesia regarding the place of the deep influences of religion in the fabric of public life, from family to church to corporate and economic life. He suggests that we need to recover a metaphysical-moral vision that will give guidance to the structures of society and provide meaning and value to the various sectors comprising civil society. Stackhouse argues that this kind of theology is not merely confessional but "engages philosophy and science, ethics and the analysis of social life, to find out which kinds of faith enhance life."[73] In several places, Stackhouse argues that the interaction among religious insight, philosophical wisdom, and social analysis is a key factor in the development of a public theology.[74]

Nine key themes are central to Stackhouse's approach to public theology. The first is creation. We must recognize that reality as created by God points us to a reality beyond ourselves to whom we are accountable and who serves as the ultimate reference point for how we are to structure our lives together. The second is liberation. This involves social change that is a response to a just God who governs history and will eventually rectify patterns of oppression. Vocation

72. Max L. Stackhouse, *Public Theology and Political Economy: Christian Stewardship in Modern Society* (Grand Rapids: Eerdmans, 1987), xi.

73. Max L. Stackhouse, "Public Theology and Ethical Judgment," *Theology Today* 54 (July 1997): 168.

74. For example, see ibid.; and Max L. Stackhouse, Peter L. Berger, Dennis P. McCann, and M. Douglas Meeks, *Christian Social Ethics in a Global Era*, Abingdon Press Studies in Christian Ethics and Economic Life 1 (Nashville: Abingdon, 1995).

is third. We must not only reflect on the chief ends of our lives as individuals but also examine how we should order our life together as a community and a society. What does it mean to obey God and define, obey, and enhance the specific values and purposes proper to each sector of common life?

Covenant is a fourth theme. This focuses on how we are to live out our vocations responsibly. It leads to accountability in social relationships and holds that God sets terms and limits for our lives together to which we are subject. It is the community-ordering side of vocation. The fifth theme is moral law, which attempts to answer the question "Is there right and wrong?" and asserts that there are universally valid moral laws rooted in God. In an attempt to discern these laws, it is easier to discover the negatives (do not murder, rape, steal, etc.) than the positives.

Sin is sixth. This theme involves reflection on and recognition of the human tendency to betray ourselves, our neighbors, our world, and God. It also involves consideration of the distortion, brokenness, corruption, and failure in every sociohistorical context. The seventh theme is freedom. This theme deals with the question of how such sinful distortion is possible under a sovereign God and also addresses humanity's dual capacity for being genuinely human and genuinely licentious and traitorous. The eighth theme is ecclesiology. This focuses on the free exercise and critique of religion, the recognition of the rights of other religious groups to propagate their views of sin and salvation in private and public affairs to the people. This theme is rooted in the "free-church" tradition and encourages religious institutions to set forth and clarify the metaphysical moral meanings that give purpose and structure to life beyond particular group loyalties. A confidence in persuasion is implicit here, the ability to persuade others regarding the merits of a particular confessional stance.

The final theme is the Trinity. The orthodox doctrine of the Trinity conceives of reality in terms of a coherent, integrated diversity. It encourages pluralism but under a greater and final unity.[75] This doctrine also recognizes a secondary pluralism in the incarnation of Christ. This trinitarian theme points toward a radical appreciation of

75. For a specific example of this theme, see Max L. Stackhouse, "The Trinity as Public Theology: Its Truth and Justice for Free-Church, Noncredal Communities," in *Faith to Creed,* ed. S. Mark Heim (Grand Rapids: Eerdmans, 1991).

both transcendence and humanity, viewing both as true but reducing neither to the other.[76] Stackhouse uses these nine themes to clarify and communicate the justice of God in a public context and to reveal components of thought that connect to contemporary human affairs and issues of concern. He hopes that modern adaptations of these themes may provide certain clues for constructing a public theology in this postindustrial, global age.

What warrants does Stackhouse use to determine the validity of theological positions? He proposes the use of the Wesleyan quadrilateral of Scripture, tradition, reason, and experience. Stackhouse uses these four "touchstones of authority" but recasts them from an ecumenical viewpoint. He acknowledges that other traditions have scriptures, but his focus is primarily on the Bible because he finds that it is the most compatible with the depths of reason and experience (even if, e.g., Buddhist scriptures present much about reason and Hindu scriptures disclose much about experience). He understands Scripture as a book in which the inspiration of the holy can be found. He encourages a critical approach to the Bible and seeks to find in Scripture principles that are eternally true and just; principles that may need further development; and principles that will function in our context to relieve malaise and foster hope, reconciliation, forgiveness, and peace with justice. Scripture serves as a boundary line that tests contemporary claims about what is adequate as a "word for today."

Tradition reveals mistakes that have been made and corrected as Scripture has been interpreted and applied, and it should be viewed as the dynamic story of the connection between Scripture and successive encounters with the complexities of civilization.[77] Tradition may be modified over time (it is ongoing and cumulative), but it is not to be ignored. In this Stackhouse has an appreciation for the catholicity of tradition.

Reason is that which makes theological statements comprehensible. It is the deep *logos* of creation, history, and redemption. It is a tool

76. All themes taken from Stackhouse, *Public Theology and Political Economy*, 18–34.

77. In this he manifests an interest in the dynamic of the Spirit as developed in Paul Tillich, *Systematic Theology* (Chicago: University of Chicago Press, 1963); and James Luther Adams, *On Being Human Religiously: Selected Essays in Religion and Society*, ed. Max L. Stackhouse (Boston: Beacon, 1976).

for successful communication, and in a secular society in which there is widespread ignorance of Scripture and tradition, it is an important criterion in public discourse. Reason serves to demonstrate why the principles of public theology make sense in the economic, political, and social spheres as well as in metaphysical-moral senses.

Experience is a criterion that recognizes the wisdom present in the sensibilities and practice of life. A key for Stackhouse in this regard is that "public theology cannot violate the deepest emotional fabric of human existence nor the profound mores by which people make daily life bearable."[78] What public theology can do is help identify those dimensions of feelings and mores that are of common import. Further, Stackhouse envisions a public theology that is expressed in compassion and love. It must be presented in a way that does not alienate people. This is a concrete manifestation of the Spirit. Experience is a key criterion for avoiding such alienation.[79] Stackhouse believes that a public theology can be constructed using his key themes and the boundaries set by the quadrilateral.[80]

Ronald Thiemann

In *Constructing a Public Theology: The Church in a Pluralistic Culture,* Ronald Thiemann defines public theology as "faith seeking to understand the relation between Christian convictions and the broader social and cultural context within which the Christian community lives."[81] Drawing on the work of Clifford Geertz,[82] Thiemann sets forth a "thick description" of the Christian community and the contemporary context. This descriptive approach is intended to show how a theology shaped by biblical narratives and grounded in the practices and institutional life of the Christian community can provide resources that enable people of faith to regain a public voice in a

78. Stackhouse, *Public Theology and Political Economy,* 14.
79. Summarized from ibid., 4–15.
80. For more specific examples of Stackhouse's approach to public theology, see *Christian Social Ethics in a Global Era;* and Max L. Stackhouse, *Covenant and Commitments: Faith, Family, and Economic Life* (Louisville: Westminster John Knox, 1997).
81. Ronald F. Thiemann, *Constructing a Public Theology: The Church in a Pluralistic Culture* (Louisville: Westminster John Knox, 1991), 21.
82. See Clifford Geertz, "Thick Description: Toward an Interpretive Theory of Culture," in *The Interpretation of Cultures: Selected Essays* (New York: Basic Books, 1973), 10.

pluralistic culture. The key challenge is to develop a public theology that is based on the particularities of the Christian faith yet genuinely addresses issues of public significance. The goal of this descriptive approach is to identify the particular places where Christian convictions intersect with the practices that characterize contemporary public life. This is not something that can be known in advance, and the relevance of Christian convictions for public policy issues must be discovered through a process of rigorous inquiry in which faith risks genuine engagement with the forces of public life. In this element of risk, Thiemann sounds similar to David Tracy, with the key exception that Thiemann's starting point is the community of faith and not a rational demonstration or a metaphysical argument. Nevertheless, he does state that faith may have to be reshaped and some convictions may have to be jettisoned after prolonged critical inquiry and engagement with public life.[83] As implied above, Thiemann's theology is explicitly nonfoundational, eschewing general explanatory schemes and seeking to provide a justification of Christian belief specific to the faith community. It is an attempt to redescribe the internal logic of the Christian faith.

Christian identity formation is another focal point in Thiemann's approach. He argues that if the church is to form disciples (teaching dispositions, capacities, and skills), then it must attend to the public dimension of life, providing theological guidance regarding matters such as the relationship between discipleship and citizenship in a liberal democracy. One way to do this is for churches to become "schools of public virtue" that seek to form the character necessary for public life. Further, theologians must engage in careful and detailed analyses of the complex web of relations within which Christians work out their vocation of discipleship.[84]

Thiemann's approach has seven key characteristics. First, he calls for a recognition of moral and cultural pluralism. He recognizes that there is no longer a common morality or culture and seeks a path between moral relativism and cultural-religious imperialism. He encourages the practice of a positive religious pluralism. Second, he reaffirms the role of religion in public life. He seeks to debunk the notion of religion's absence from public life and to demonstrate

83. Thiemann, *Constructing a Public Theology,* 22–23.
84. Ibid., 126–28.

that questions of conviction, value, and faith should be a part of public discourse.

The recovery of religious roots is the third characteristic. Confessional public theology seeks a reversal of liberalism's accommodation to culture. Fourth, there is no single solution to the religion/public life relationship. Thiemann perceives that new models of policy development are needed, along with the development of individuals who combine prophetic vision with careful analysis of policy. This calls for new educational forms that provide ethical and theological training for public and church leaders. Thiemann believes that the church has a significant role to play in this. The fifth characteristic is a desire to have religious convictions and theological analyses impact the structure of public life and policy. Thiemann addresses the challenge of influencing the development of public policy without seeking to construct a new Christendom or lapsing into a benign moral relativism.[85]

A sixth characteristic is the acknowledgment that the biblical narratives demonstrate a way of life. In Thiemann's view, narratives such as that of the unnamed woman at Bethany are coherent and reveal the pattern of discipleship, which is the way of the cross.[86] The seventh and final characteristic is the belief that worship helps shape public responsibility. Public theology involves rediscovering the link between worship and education and recognizing (from 1 Cor. 12, which speaks of diversity in the body of Christ) that the church can model an approach to life in a pluralistic society. It is also vital to remember that the church's most important service is to be a community of hope.[87]

Anyone familiar with the Yale postliberals can probably recognize that Thiemann's approach is, using George Lindbeck's categories, "cultural linguistic." This is an anthropological, community-specific approach that Thiemann uses to provide his "thick description." He and his fellow postliberals attempt to articulate a public theology that retains the identity of the church in a pluralistic context and that tries to argue from an explicitly confessional stance.[88]

85. Characteristics 1–5 are summarized from ibid., 38–43.

86. Ibid., 63–71.

87. Ibid., 112–25.

88. A specific example of Thiemann's approach to public theology is his *Religion in Public Life: A Dilemma for Democracy* (Washington, D.C.: Georgetown University Press, 1996).

Both Stackhouse and Thiemann desire to see the public impact of theology, though they differ fundamentally regarding the public value of a purely confessional stance. Both approaches to public theology have designs on shaping history as it moves forward, but the question remains as to which approach better embodies the pneumatologically derived approach that this present book aims to articulate. Where does the approach of Abraham Kuyper fit? Was his approach to public engagement primarily apologetic, or did his theological rationale require the maintenance of a distinctive Christian identity, belief, and practice? Is there any common area of discourse and interaction between Christians and others in the public realm? To an introduction of Kuyper this work now turns.

Abraham Kuyper, the Public Theologian

The final strand in the thread is the person and work of Abraham Kuyper. Kuyper could be called many things (e.g., politician, journalist, churchman, professor), but the label "public theologian" encompasses his diverse roles. Born in 1837 in Maassluis, he was the son of Jan Frederik Kuyper, a minister in the Nederlandse Hervormde Kerk (the Reformed state church in the Netherlands), and grew up in a large family. He went to gymnasium (an equivalent to high school) in Leiden from 1849 to 1855 and enrolled in the university in Leiden to study literature and theology. Though raised in an orthodox home, Kuyper was influenced by the spirit of the time and adopted the perspective of modern theologians who restated traditional Christian doctrines in a manner that was palatable to the intelligentsia. Kuyper's primary influence at Leiden was J. H. Scholten, a mesmerizing personality and the "grand master of Dutch Modernism."[89] Scholten's influence would remain a factor in Kuyper's thought.

In 1860, Kuyper completed a treatise (in Latin) comparing John Calvin and John a Lasco, a Polish reformer, for a competition sponsored by the University of Groningen. His work was awarded the highest honors, and he rewrote it as his doctoral thesis. Though he won the prize, unfortunately he had worked himself to total exhaustion. For the majority of 1861, he was unable to do anything other

89. Louis Praamsma, *Let Christ Be King: Reflections on the Life and Times of Abraham Kuyper* (Jordan Station, Ont.: Paideia, 1985), 36.

than sit with a book. While recovering, he read Charlotte Yonge's *Heir of Redclyffe*, a book sent to him by Johanna Hendrika Schaay, his fiancée. While reading this book, which contrasts the lives of two young men, one arrogant (Philip) and the other humble (Guy), Kuyper found his own life challenged by the climax (the humbling of the arrogant Philip and the exaltation of the dying Guy). Starkly recognizing his need for a changed life, Kuyper experienced what George Puchinger calls an "ethical" conversion.[90] In a letter to Johanna, Kuyper described it:

> Things were not right with me. I was too self-satisfied, too ostentatious, too selfish, too much lacking in nobility, too little a child of God. For years I have deceived myself and told myself that I did good. I rocked my conscience and my naive soul asleep. I no longer knew what sin was, I never had remorse. . . . I could no longer control myself, it was already half past twelve—I was alone in my study, went upstairs, fell down on my knees and prayed, long and passionately. I had not done that for years. . . . Did I search for God? No, it was virtue, a concept, an ideal, that I raved about, that fit with my ambition, that kept me standing and brought me this far. But I did not know God, because the confession of sins and the deep, inner remorse of a broken heart were still strange to me, they did not live in my heart. If I had written to somebody else but you, my dear Jo, I would have torn up my letter fearing that the confession of my struggle would have been interpreted as another expression of my ostentatious heart; but you won't think so, I know that.[91]

This ethical conversion was a private matter between Kuyper, Johanna, and God and was not shared with anyone else at the time. It is important to note that while Kuyper recognized a need for a change in his approach to life, there was not yet a change in his confessional stance. Upon his full recovery from exhaustion, he married Johanna and took a parish in the rural village of Beesd. While serving in this parish, Kuyper experienced his confessional conversion and recognized the need for public theology.

Among the parishioners at Beesd was a group of malcontents who had ceased attending church in protest against the modern theology taught in state churches. They met together in small groups instead

90. George Puchinger, *Abraham Kuyper: His Early Journey of Faith*, ed. George Harinck, trans. Simone Kennedy (Amsterdam: VU University Press, 1998), 17–20.
91. Ibid., 18–19.

of attending church. Kuyper had been advised to ignore them, but he decided to venture out and meet these people. Kuyper offered the following description of the malcontents:

> I heard that there was a small group of malcontents in the flock, but the rumors about these know-it-alls were more for ill than good. They were a bunch of cantankerous, proud eccentrics who "make life miserable for every minister." Besides, most of them were of such low social status that it was deemed best not to worry about them but to ignore them, just as previous ministers had done. But I found it impossible to do so.[92]

The malcontents also had a negative view of Kuyper. They perceived him as a representative of the state church who had an immature orthodoxy. In their eyes, he knew little of the historic Reformed faith.

One of these malcontent parishioners, Pietje Baltus, initially refused to shake Kuyper's hand when he made a pastoral visit. She eventually shook his hand but made it clear that she disapproved of Kuyper's modern theology. Rather than being insulted, Kuyper was intrigued by the fact that Baltus and the malcontents had an interest in spiritual matters, knowledge of the Bible, and a well-organized worldview. Kuyper knew he did not know nearly as much about orthodox Reformed faith as these "simple" people. What he found most interesting about them was that "here spoke a heart that had a history and life-experiences, its own observations and emotions, and that not only had them but knew them."[93]

This attraction led him back after his initial visitation, and he soon began to meet with them regularly. His original intent was to debate these people, but he found himself primarily in the role of a listener. In spite of his desires, these people made no compromise on their position, and he had to decide whether to resist them or to join them in a "principled recognition of sovereign grace." Kuyper did not oppose them and wrote of it in this manner:

> I did not oppose them and I still thank God that I made that choice. Their unremitting perseverance has become the blessing of my heart,

92. Abraham Kuyper, "Confidentially," in *Abraham Kuyper: A Centennial Reader,* ed. James D. Bratt (Grand Rapids: Eerdmans, 1998), 55.
93. Ibid., 55–56.

the rise of the morning star in my life. I had been convicted but had not yet found the Word of reconciliation. That they brought me, with their imperfect language, in that absolute form which alone can give rest to my soul: in the worship and adoration of a God who works all things, both the willing and the working, according to his good pleasure![94]

Puchinger views this decision as Kuyper's second conversion, saying, "No one can understand the Kuyper he became without realizing that his decisive *confessional* transformation was not an academic conversion, but a religious one, which happened through the talks with the simplest farmers and laborers of Beesd, who pointed him the way spiritually."[95]

When did the turn to public theology occur? Many scholars argue that it developed as Kuyper formulated a complete response to the malcontents. He decided not to join their fellowships and become a full participant in this form of conventicle pietism.[96] While their staunch Calvinism was the spiritual antidote and salve Kuyper needed,[97] he felt that more was needed. He said, "You can see that they didn't give me enough. The thinking of our era differs from that of Gomarus, and their world of thought was literally still rooted in the days immediately following the Reformation."[98] Kuyper recognized that this orthodoxy had to be restated, reformulated in contemporary language. Kuyper, furthermore, was not satisfied to leave Calvinist orthodoxy in the meeting rooms of these simple people (he affectionately referred to such people as

94. Ibid., 56.

95. Puchinger, *Abraham Kuyper,* 26–27.

96. Though Kuyper does not refer to the malcontents as pietists, Bratt describes their fellowships as conventicle pietism. See Bratt, *Abraham Kuyper,* 9. It also seems that the malcontents did not label themselves pietists, but in spite of this, a description of their faith and practice fits the label "pietists," albeit a Reformed variety. For a description of pietist characteristics and an argument concerning the breadth (e.g., Lutheran *and* Reformed) of pietism, see F. Ernest Stoeffler, "Pietism: Its Message, Early Manifestation, and Significance," *Covenant Quarterly* 32 (February/March 1976): 4–24.

97. Bratt describes the malcontents' contribution as providing the absolute certainty of faith that Kuyper needed to go along with the modernist consistency he learned from Scholten. See Bratt, *Abraham Kuyper,* 9.

98. Kuyper, "Confidentially," 56. Franciscus Gomarus was a professor of theology at Leiden who led the attack on Jacobus Arminius and his followers that resulted in the Synod of Dordt, 1618–19. The pietist malcontents at Beesd were essentially purists who longed for the Calvinism of Dordt.

the *kleine luyden*).[99] It had to influence public life.[100] Puchinger describes Kuyper's sense of mission:

> Kuyper was born again, but he did not consider his life's fulfillment to preach his religion to others. Otherwise he would have continued to be a minister, he would have been satisfied to stay in Beesd, as was expected from every pastor and priest. No, Kuyper wanted to represent something else as journalist, political agitator, member of Parliament, professor, social lobbyist, and prime minister. He wanted to point to the fact that, even in a neutral state, the public character of religion needed to be taken into account. Not only in education, but also more generally in the opportunity for every religion—Catholic or Reformed, orthodox or liberal, humanistic or non-Christian—to be *expressed* and *respected*.[101]

After his transformation at Beesd, Kuyper launched into a life of public theology.[102] Though he had moved beyond his mentor

99. "Like no one before him he took the simple people by the hand. He did not proudly expose their naiveté and ignorance, did not mock or ridicule them, he did not subject them to irony, torment, and opposition, as was customary at that time and widely applauded by scholars, journalists and other civilized people. Instead he healed them from many weaknesses and patiently educated them. He understood that however much he might have accomplished, he could never forsake or abandon these people who had transformed him. . . . For his whole life he would remain faithful to the orthodox people. He reeducated them, pulled them out of their backwardness to participate in the public life of the church, state and society" (Puchinger, *Abraham Kuyper*, 28–29).

100. An interesting way to look at Kuyper's launch into public theology is to consider labeling it a "better pietism" than that practiced at Beesd. While the term *pietism* is not often used in connection with Kuyper, it may be valid to suggest that the phrase "better" or "transformed" pietism accurately describes Kuyper's attempt not only to recontextualize but also to manifest publicly the faith commitment of the *kleine luyden*.

101. Puchinger, *Abraham Kuyper*, 27–28. The implication of Kuyper's vision of public theology is one that is not satisfied with confessionalism alone. For him it is of paramount importance that religious convictions move outside the confessional enclave and into public life.

102. Jasper Vree is a scholar who offers a different view of Kuyper's "turn" to public theology. He argues that one can see Kuyper's concerns for matters such as church, state, and family in some of the earliest sermons Kuyper preached at Beesd. He also argues that a key factor in elaborating his public theological concerns was the departure of Allard Pierson (a colleague of Kuyper's) from the Reformed Church. In sermons that addressed the Pierson issue, Vree finds Kuyper articulating his views on the position of the church in state and society. As the title of his article reveals, Vree suggests that more

Scholten in his confessional theology, Kuyper followed his mentor in method. As James Bratt notes, "He certainly did absorb Scholten's example of bold undertakings and his method of principial consistency—that is, assuming a fixed starting point and building upon it logically and fearlessly. He also followed Scholten back to the founding documents of the Reformed tradition in search of its first principles and in admiration of its iron spirit."[103] Though he was more theologically conservative than Scholten, Kuyper insisted that first principles be carried through to every area of life, a reflection of the impact of his education. Kuyper's approach to public engagement was framed by the problems raised by the movements and thinkers of the modern era. Like everyone, Kuyper was embedded in his context, but he was not so determined by his context that he was not able to transcend it, as a close reading of his work reveals.

As a living expression of public theology, Kuyper sought to engage the challenges of the modern era. He was unique in that he was an intellectual who led a popular movement.[104] In his long career, perhaps his most fruitful era was 1890 to 1905. During that period, Kuyper gave a significant address at the First Christian Social Congress (originally titled "The Social Question and the Christian Religion," a modern translation by James Skillen is titled *The Problem of Poverty*); published significant essays such as "Christianity and Art," "Maranatha," and "The Blurring of the Boundaries"; published his scholarly work *The Encyclopedia of Sacred Theology*; wrote a series on common grace from 1895 to 1901 (published in three volumes from 1901 to 1905); gave the Stone Lectures on Calvinism at Princeton Theological Seminary in 1898; and served as prime minister of the Netherlands from 1901 to 1905. This period was Kuyper's zenith. His contributions during this era reveal his mature approach to public theology, an approach that, we will see in chapter 3, was intimately linked to the work of the Spirit in creation.

---

research needs to be done on this early period in Kuyper. See J. Vree, "More Pierson and Mesmer, and Less Pietje Baltus: Kuyper's Ideas on Church, State, Society, and Culture during the First Years of His Ministry (1863–1866)," in *Kuyper Reconsidered: Aspects of His Life and Work,* ed. Cornelis van der Kooi and Jan de Bruijn, VU Studies on Protestant History (Amsterdam: VU Uitgeverij, 1999), 299–309.

103. Bratt, *Abraham Kuyper,* 8.
104. Ibid., 2.

CONCLUSION

The central aim of this book is twofold: first, to reveal the inter-related character of the strands of a thread comprised of pneumatology linked to creation and history, public theology, and the work of Abraham Kuyper; and second, to articulate a contemporary formulation of Kuyperian public theology rooted in the Holy Spirit's role in creation and history. The core of this book is Abraham Kuyper, who embodies public theology and articulates a view of the work of the Spirit in creation.

This introductory survey has revealed several approaches to cosmic pneumatology that address the relationship between creation (understood as nature or the biophysical order) and the Spirit. Many of these have a direct relationship with some form of earthly concern (e.g., Moltmann, Müller-Fahrenholz, and Wallace). Among the issues that must be addressed are the conception of the Spirit/earth relationship, the implications of that relationship for human engagement of creation, and the articulation of a contemporary cosmic pneumatology (this includes developing a pneumatological logic along the lines of Van Ruler and McIntyre) in a Kuyperian vein.

Furthermore, the survey of public theology reveals the Christian concern to impact the path of an increasingly complex society with theological convictions. For this book, a key question concerns the position of Kuyperian public theology. In particular, does an emphasis on the antithesis between Christian and non-Christian approaches to public life make Kuyper's approach confessional, or does the emphasis on common grace (and the matter of Kuyper's own political practice) make the approach more apologetic in cast? The path forward involves articulating Kuyper's public theology, the relationship between common grace and cosmic pneumatology, and, finally, a contemporary reformulation of creation stewardship as public theology. This will be more than a mere restatement of Kuyper's approach, for recontextualization requires more than cutting and pasting Kuyperian slogans from his era into ours. In his spirit, the following recontextualization gives serious consideration to the current context and endeavors to offer a faithful translation of Kuyperian public theology for twenty-first-century eyes.

2

ABRAHAM KUYPER'S PUBLIC THEOLOGY AT ITS ZENITH (1890–1905)

SETTING THE STAGE

Although this chapter's primary focus is Kuyper's work dating from 1890 to 1905, it begins first with reference to seminal works and events in the preceding decades, in particular, Kuyper's role in leading the Anti-Revolutionary Party and in the founding of the Free University of Amsterdam. These two items are significant in their relation to the theory and practice of Kuyper's public theology.

Kuyper and the Anti-Revolutionary Party

Abraham Kuyper initially entered the political world as a journalist. In 1872, he established *De Standaard* (*The Standard*), a daily newspaper. As editor, Kuyper wrote editorials that argued for the use of divine ordinances in national affairs. This was precipitated by the need for a Christian option in politics. Kuyper found that both the Conservative and the Liberal parties were secular in principle and practice. The regnant Liberal Party was seeking to diminish the impact of religion in culture and society as it had already done in politics.

A dominant secularism existed throughout Europe, and the Netherlands was no exception. This secularism was rooted in the beliefs of the French Revolution and the Enlightenment that had spawned a progressive humanism. The status quo was atheistic unbelief, which meant a greatly diminished role for religion in public life. Religion was primarily privatized.

Kuyper sought another way, in which one could see the effects of the Reformed faith in all areas of life. As a journalist, he wrote the following in *De Standaard* in 1873:

> God has spoken. There is a revelation of His will which we have in God's Word. On this basis we demand that the pronouncement of God's Word be obeyed in each clash of principles. Human inference or discretion is only to be decisive where God's Word is unclear. Everybody agrees that human insight must yield to God's pronouncements. The disagreement begins because our opponents do not believe God Himself has spoken while we confess that He has spoken. The Gospel versus the Revolution! This is the conviction that we must be able to declare in order to awaken the proper type of belief. We only ask for this right, but this is what we are denied.[1]

Kuyper spoke of a "clash of principles," which would characterize his engagement with secular systems of thought throughout his life. The lines were clearly drawn, and Kuyper argued for the right to bring a revelation-based perspective into public life. He did more than write as a journalist, however. In 1874, he was elected to the Second Chamber of the Dutch Parliament, and in 1879, he became the chairman of the new Anti-Revolutionary Party.

In Kuyper's leadership of the Anti-Revolutionary Party, two pertinent developments were significant for his public theology. The first was a relationship between Kuyper and Herman Schaepman. Kuyper's friendship with this Catholic clergyman and member of Parliament led to the Anti-Revolutionary-Catholic political coalition that resulted in Kuyper's ascendence to prime minister in 1901.[2] The coalition developed around the issue of education, for both the Catholics and

---

1. Quoted in McKendree R. Langley, *The Practice of Political Spirituality: Episodes from the Public Career of Abraham Kuyper, 1879–1918* (Jordan Station, Ont.: Paideia, 1984), 12. Langley does not provide any information regarding a title or translation. He gives only a date of June 7, 1873.

2. Ibid., 32.

the Anti-Revolutionaries sought a pluralistic educational system that would allow confessional groups to form their own schools. The second development was more ideological. In *De Standaard*, Kuyper wrote a series of articles that articulated a theological rationale for the Anti-Revolutionaries' involvement in public life. The argument was rooted in the "ordinances of God." Kuyper explained that from a Reformed perspective, one

> can distinguish a dual confession in the use of this concept: 1) that ordinances, indeed, divine ordinances, do exist, and 2) that there is a way that we can come to know these ordinances. The first confession touches on the principle of the Anti-Revolution itself. The second pertains to the distinction between ourselves and related movements.[3]

Kuyper explained that in contrast to the social contract theory and varieties of positivism, the Anti-Revolutionaries believed that there are real, divine ordinances built into creation by God that can be discovered through experience. These laws are discovered not merely through biblical exegesis or spiritual reflection but in the process of governance. He stated:

> We regard as incontrovertible the assertion that the laws governing life reveal themselves spontaneously in life. In the very process of painting and sketching and performing and sculpting our artists discovered the laws for the artistic enterprise. And it enters no one's mind to consult the Bible or ecclesiastical authorities when it comes to learning what the purpose of art is. (We are not talking here about judging the moral character of art objects.) The same is true of the laws which govern our thinking, the laws which govern commerce, and the laws which govern industry. We learn to know the laws of thought by thinking. By doing business we discover the art of commerce. Industry blazes its own path. The same is true for political life. To deny this truth is to fall short of respect for the Creator.[4]

While making this argument, Kuyper added a significant qualification. The reality of sin prevents the unencumbered discovery of the divine ordinances. If sin did not exist, the observation of life itself

---

3. Abraham Kuyper, "The Antirevolutionary Program," in *Political Order and the Plural Structure of Society,* ed. James Skillen and Rockne M. McCarthy (Atlanta: Scholars Press, 1991), 242.
4. Ibid., 246.

would be sufficient for the task. In Kuyper's Reformed perspective, all of life has been tainted by sin, and this condition yields frustration for those who would attempt to discover the ordinances through observation alone. This leads to the question of how sin-tainted humans can discover and recognize the divine ordinances.

Kuyper responded to this dilemma with a solution that surprised his critics. He was quick to state that the methodology for finding the divine ordinances did not require a cessation of the observation of life, nor did it mandate the adoption of Scripture as a code of Christian law for the state. In addition, contrary to Anabaptist and Quaker viewpoints, which posited a radical distinction between the Christian community and the rest of the world, it was wrong to consider the political organization of states a necessary evil rooted in the reality of sin. In Kuyper's view, "If we considered the political life of the nations as something unholy, unclean and wrong in itself, it would lie outside of human nature. Then the state would have to be seen as a purely external means of compulsion, and every attempt to discover even a trace of God's ordinances in our own nature would be absurd."[5] If such a situation did exist, the only way humans could receive the standards for external means of discipline would be through special revelation. This would lead one to conclude, then, that the absence of special revelation would leave nothing in the world worthy of observation because sin and distortion would prevail, as in societies that lack Christian influence. In contrast to such a pessimistic perspective on discovering divine ordinances, Kuyper stated:

> However, if we open the works of Calvin, Bullinger, Beza and Marnix van St. Aldegonde, it becomes obvious that Calvinism consciously chooses sides against this viewpoint. The experiences of the states of antiquity, the practical wisdom of their laws, and the deep insight of their statesmen and philosophers is held in esteem by these men, and these are cited in support of their own affirmations and consciously related to the ordinances of God. The earnest intent of the political life of many nations can be explained in terms of the principles of justice and morality that spoke in their consciences. They cannot be explained simply as blindness brought on by the Evil One; on the contrary, in the excellence of the political efforts we encounter a divine ray of light.[6]

5. Ibid., 249.
6. Ibid.

Kuyper maintained that the rules of political life are built into the created order and that even non-Christians can articulate approaches to national life that reflect divine principles.

Kuyper also distanced the Anti-Revolutionary approach from a Roman Catholic view in which the state must act in accordance with the revelation-derived rules pronounced by the church. Though many critics assumed that this was indeed the Anti-Revolutionary approach, Kuyper argued that such an approach is improper because the state should not be subject to the direct control of the church. There is no problem with *influence,* but the church "may not establish rules that would bind the state."[7] A key reason for this is that the church does not possess the appropriate knowledge of matters such as history and politics. While the church may understand biblical revelation, it does not have the expertise required for the formation and development of political principles. The proper relationship between the church and the state is one of "mutually mediated contact only through the persons who stand in relation to both."[8] Christians trained in matters of statecraft should set the political agenda. If they are given the appropriate spiritual direction, whereby they have the conviction that their entire lives are bound by the Word of God, then they will be a spiritual influence that shapes political opinion. For Kuyper, this approach allowed a place for divine revelation to influence the state without direct legislation from the biblical text.

One question remained: How does a statesman acquire knowledge of the divine ordinances? Kuyper acknowledged that this is not a simple task. It requires the ability to derive scriptural principles as well as the acumen to draw principles of political order from ethnology and history. This interdisciplinary expertise must then form a coherent unity within the thought of the statesman. For Kuyper, the doctrine of the incarnation, in which divinity and humanity permeate each other, exemplified this approach, though politically one speaks of "a mutual inter-penetration of the givens of God's Word and the givens derived from a study of nations."[9] A significant implication Kuyper drew from this is that it is impossible to create a manual for Christian political theory that suffices for all times and nations. Recognizing that times change and nations differ in character, Kuyper

7. Ibid., 252.
8. Ibid.
9. Ibid., 254.

argued that only the principles are eternally valid. What are some of these principles? Kuyper's examples included justice, authority (divine and earthly), and the struggle for freedom and progress. In addition, he argued that Scripture offers the nation of Israel as an example of a gifted nation that found happiness or destruction depending on its adherence to these principles.[10] Once these principles are combined with knowledge of history and politics, then it is possible to move toward discovery of the divine ordinances. Kuyper stated:

> Standing thus on firm ground in contemplation of these basic principles, knowing what man is, knowing what a nation is and the purpose of the nations, knowing the source of justice and authority, knowing too where the claim to freedom and progress derives its impulse, he possesses the compass that points the way across the tossing seas even when there is no land in sight. The formulation of these principles must be the fruit of his own inner life. He himself must assimilate these principles into his own person and life so that he may find the thoughts, the expressions, the words, in which these principles can be embodied, not as from a code-book to which some would demote Scripture, but from faith which takes up the Word of God into itself.[11]

The political principles, once discovered, are not to be left alone but refined with each subsequent generation. The principles should be used to critique the aspects of national life and politics that are contrary to them, and the Anti-Revolutionary should seek to present historical proof that the principles have been tested and found durable. An interesting point for public theology follows: Kuyper encouraged his followers to "seek that point-of-contact in the conscience of both the citizen and statesman by which respect for these principles can be revived; and to sever every form of cooperation which would remove the question of principles from the order of the day."[12] The first statement lays bare Kuyper's contention that there is a level at which the principles derived from the divine ordinances can be comprehended. He does not say how much comprehension is possible, and he moves on to call for vigilance in keeping matters of principle central to the political discussion. Yet the statement reveals that the earlier Kuyper was

10. Ibid., 255–56.
11. Ibid., 256.
12. Ibid.

the one who at the very least articulated a public theology that had apologetic aspects.

For Kuyper, the reality of divine ordinances made Christian political engagement possible, though without ecclesiastical control. The distinction Kuyper made between the appropriate "spheres" of authority in the realms of church and state[13] serves as the foundation for the next significant antecedent: the inauguration of the Free University of Amsterdam.

Kuyper, the Free University, and Sphere Sovereignty

In 1880, Kuyper gave the inaugural speech for the Free University of Amsterdam (*Vrije Universiteit*),[14] an institution of higher education that taught not only theology but also science, philosophy, literature, and medicine. The objective of this institution was to provide an approach to higher education that was rooted in a Reformed worldview.[15] The heart of the address lies in its title, *Souvreiniteit in Eigen Kring* (translated as "Sovereignty in the Distinct Spheres of Human Life" or, more commonly, "Sphere Sovereignty"). Kuyper's objective was to argue for a form of pluralism in society rooted in God's sovereignty and the structure of creation itself. Kuyper argued, in contrast to those who viewed the state as possessing unlimited rule, that only God and the Messiah possess such ultimate sovereignty. Then came Kuyper's step toward pluralism:

> But here is the glorious principle of Freedom! This perfect Sovereignty of the *sinless* Messiah at the same time directly denies and challenges all absolute sovereignty among *sinful* men on earth, and does so by dividing all of life into *separate spheres*, each with its own sovereignty.[16]

13. See ibid., 255. "No earthly authority can ever assert itself contrary to the obedience we owe God. Similarly, this (earthly) authority can never nullify the authority with which others are clothed in their own spheres. The state cannot legitimately assert its authority over against the father, nor a prince over against the rights of other governing bodies and the people within their spheres of competence."

14. For a detailed approach to the origin of the Free University of Amsterdam, see Wayne A. Kobes, "Sphere Sovereignty and the University: Theological Foundations of Abraham Kuyper's View of the University and Its Role in Society" (Ph.D. diss., Florida State University, 1993).

15. Louis Praamsma, *Let Christ Be King: Reflections on the Life and Times of Abraham Kuyper* (Jordan Station, Ont.: Paideia, 1985), 73–76.

16. Abraham Kuyper, "Sphere Sovereignty," in *Abraham Kuyper: A Centennial Reader*, ed. James D. Bratt (Grand Rapids: Eerdmans, 1998), 467.

For Kuyper, there is a sovereignty derivative of God in the great complexity that comprises human existence. In the realms of politics, art, and education (to name a few),[17] laws of life exist that are specific to the particular area. Further, because each sphere "comprises its own domain, each has its own Sovereign within its bounds."[18] As noted above, this view of pluralism made it possible to argue that government, church, and education should all operate under their own authority.

For Kuyper, there were two objectives in making the case for sphere sovereignty. First, he wanted to make the argument, in terms of *structural* pluralism, that education had the right to operate free of government intervention. Second, he also wanted to make the case for *worldview* pluralism. He asserted that Christians had the right to operate their own confessionally based institutions in a context that had grown hostile to the Reformed faith throughout the nineteenth century. Regarding worldview pluralism, Kuyper said:

> Shall we pretend to grow from the selfsame root that which, according to the express pronouncement of Jesus' divine self-consciousness, is rooted entirely differently? We shall *not* risk it, ladies and gentlemen! Rather, considering that something begins from principle and that a distinct entity takes rise from a distinct principle, we shall maintain a distinct sovereignty for our own principle and for that of our opponents across the whole sphere of thought. That is to say, as from their principle and by a method appropriate to it they erect a house of knowledge that glitters but does not entice us, so we too from our principle and by its corresponding method will let our own trunk shoot up whose branches, leaves, and blossoms are nourished with its own sap.[19]

It is important to observe that Kuyper's proposal made room for institutions of a variety of worldviews, not just the Reformed perspective. It is also vital to note that Kuyper's structural pluralism was not the same as subsidiarity, a Catholic view of social order. As James Skillen and Rockne McCarthy note in their introduction to Kuyper's essay:

17. Ibid. Kuyper does not give a number of spheres, saying, "The name or image is unimportant, so long as we recognize that there are in life as many spheres as there are constellations in the sky."

18. Ibid.

19. Ibid., 484–85.

Kuyper's argument is different from that of "subsidiarity," which stresses a natural, *vertical* hierarchy of responsibilities in social life along with the rightful autonomy of the various parts within the societal "whole" which the state governs. In the subsidiarity argument the state is charged with the protection and promotion of the common good of the whole society, whereas Kuyper is suggesting a more *horizontal* concept of social spheres, among which the state has less encompassing responsibility.[20]

Kuyper's approach placed God above everything, and below him the various social spheres were on the same level, interacting with one another like cogwheels and yielding "the rich, multifaceted multiformity of human life."[21] Sphere sovereignty provided Kuyper and his followers with the opportunity and the encouragement to engage the public realm. It inspired Christians to be good stewards of society as well as the church while keeping ecclesiastical authority from dictating public policy. For Kuyper, there was no way that Christians could stay out of public life, as the most famous quotation from his speech reveals:

> Oh, no single piece of our mental world is to be hermetically sealed off from the rest, and there is not a square inch in the whole domain of our human existence over which Christ, who is Sovereign over *all*, does not cry: "Mine!"[22]

Kuyper's Anti-Revolutionary activities (his friendship with a Catholic politician and his provision of a theological rationale for Anti-Revolutionary participation in politics) and his apologetic for the existence of the Free University of Amsterdam were of great significance to Kuyper's public theology. Strategically, he was willing to make an alliance with another confessional group to achieve common goals, and theologically, he sought to articulate a Reformed approach to life outside the church. His arguments concerning the ordinances of creation and the divinely based reality of pluralism[23] were fundamental to his public discourse

20. Kuyper, "Antirevolutionary Program," 241.
21. Kuyper, "Sphere Sovereignty," 468.
22. Ibid., 488.
23. One should not confuse the distinction between the two forms of pluralism for which Kuyper argues. As Harry Van Dyke notes in a review, "Structural (or ontological) pluralism, after all, is anchored in sphere sovereignty as laid down by the Creator, whereas worldview (or confessional) pluralism derives from differences in

and public activities. Throughout his career, Kuyper often referred to these two core theological ideas, and their application was often on display. To state it differently, Kuyper constantly argued that it was a Christian responsibility to discover and implement creation ordinances. Sphere sovereignty was one such divinely based reality that necessitated Christian engagement in the public square. The next section treats some key examples of Kuyper's public theology from 1890 to 1905.

KUYPER'S PUBLIC THEOLOGY ON DISPLAY

"Maranatha"

On May 12, 1891, Kuyper addressed the Anti-Revolutionary Party congress in Utrecht. The speech was given at a time when the Anti-Revolutionary Party found itself at a definitive moment. An election was at hand,[24] and the party had to decide which path to take in the face of social strains brought on by industrialization.[25]

As indicated by the title, the speech reflected on the impact of Christian eschatology on politics. Kuyper stated:

> The *destination* of a journey always determines the *road* you have to take. If for you and me that destination is wrapped up in the final catastrophe which is scheduled to occur when Jesus returns to this

---

humans' response to the Creator. . . . It is true—to return to the connection perceived in 1880—that Kuyper's case for a university free of church and state (structural pluralism) coincided with his defense of Christians to own and operate such a university bound to the Word of God (worldview pluralism). But the twin arguments must not be telescoped. They are not intrinsically connected; each stands on its own, requiring separate appraisal" (Harry Van Dyke, review of *Creating a Christian Worldview: Abraham Kuyper's Lectures on Calvinism,* by Peter S. Heslam, *Calvin Theological Journal* 33 [November 1998]: 506–7).

24. In 1887, the Mackay cabinet came into power with a majority coalition of Roman Catholics and Anti-Revolutionaries. They passed a bill that permitted state aid to religious schools and a labor bill that mandated state protection of vulnerable workers, but there were problems in the cabinet over an Anti-Revolutionary proposal to outlaw the purchase of exemptions from military service (this was opposed by the Catholics and precipitated the election of 1891). See Langley, *Practice of Political Spirituality,* 39–45; and Bratt's introductory comments to "Maranatha," in *Abraham Kuyper,* 205. A synopsis of the school funding issue, itself a significant exercise in public theology, can be found in Kobes, "Sphere Sovereignty and the University," 41–45; and James E. McGoldrick, *Abraham Kuyper: God's Renaissance Man* (Auburn, Mass.: Evangelical Press, 2000), 52–56.

25. See Bratt's introductory comments to "Maranatha," in *Abraham Kuyper.*

earth, the cry of *Maranatha* is the crossroads where our road and that of our opponents diverge. To them the return of the Lord is an illusion hardly worth the laughter of ridicule; to us it is the glorious end of history—also the history of our national existence—which we invoke with the laughter of a holy joy. To plunge immediately into the purpose of our convention: To us it is the decisive fact of the future by which not only our *spiritual* life but also our *political* course of conduct is utterly controlled.[26]

Kuyper went on to argue that his adversaries (Conservatives, Liberals, Radicals, and Socialists) had no deep recognition of the divinely appointed end of history, nor did they acknowledge the divine authority in politics in the present. In contrast, orthodox Christians acknowledge the kingship of Christ and the final destiny of the world and should consider the pursuit and promotion of political action that best reflect this conviction.

Before naming a course of action, Kuyper noted the eschatological theme of the escalation of anti-Christian sociopolitical activity that will precede the return of Christ. Where did he see this tendency? He pointed to the French Revolution, which sought to dethrone God and assert human autonomy. This revolution led to an anti-Christian worldview that had significant influence in Holland, though Kuyper stated that he did not believe the revolution itself was the final revolt against God. What concerned him was that his opponents shared the same "disastrous principle," one that was not rooted in God. This led him to a call for action:

Only one thing the cry of *Maranatha* has irrevocably instilled in you: you may not accede to their counsel. You may not join them or connive with them. Nor may you abandon the country to them. Rather, all those who love Christ and await his return from heaven must heartily unite with all sincere believers in the land to resist their philosophy and to rescue the country from their pernicious influence. And this you must do—do you confess it with me?—not by might nor by power but only in a lawful way driven by the Spirit of the Lord alone.[27]

26. Abraham Kuyper, "Maranatha," in *Abraham Kuyper,* 207–8.
27. Ibid., 213. At this point, one might inquire as to what Kuyper meant when he invoked the Spirit's power. Is this to be perceived as only sanctifying influence, or does it include the cosmic Spirit, which is preserving the creation so that Christians can engage the public realm?

Kuyper perceived a nation at stake, and his call extended to all Christians. It is clear that he viewed engagement in the national life as a significant aspect of Christian vocation. He hoped to encourage Dutch Christians to possess the "passionate desire to prepare a people who, at Christ's return, will not strive against him but welcome him with Hallelujahs."[28] In light of this objective, Kuyper attempted to create a climate that would lead to victory in the election.

Kuyper's next move in his speech was to encourage the party members by invoking the struggles of three key predecessors. William Bilderdijk, Isaac da Costa, and Groen van Prinsterer were Calvinistically inclined figures who encountered dark times in Dutch history and nevertheless took action commensurate with their convictions. Kuyper challenged his audience to resist judging the success of their principial struggle,[29] inspiring his constituency with the memory of these men:

> Who would dare say that in our country the near-miraculous has not occurred? Listen to Bilderdijk and feel in your bones the raw anguish of this solitary struggler who is ready, over and over, to bury himself under the collapsing domes of Ashdod. Hear Da Costa bewailing the plight of a nation whose ears have been stopped. Consider Groen van Prinsterer when his whole little army bolted and only the general stood firm. . . . And now: well, I'll not sketch the contrast of today, for it is not appropriate to boast. But if you compare the rich growth of the present with such a painful past and are still not moved to gratitude nor inspired with courage and hope for the future, I would almost be inclined to ask what you expected to do here among this enthusiastic corps—indeed, to ask whether from the depths of your soul you never responded to the cry of "Maranatha" with the words: "yes, come Lord Jesus!"[30]

28. Ibid.
29. "This struggle goes on for decades and centuries, and the only question is whether the influence of the Name of the Lord is shrinking or gaining over the years" (ibid., 215).
30. Ibid., 215–16. William Bilderdijk (1756–1831) was the leading Dutch poet of his time and articulated a Calvinistic and Anti-Revolutionary vision of politics and culture. Isaac da Costa (1798–1860) was a Portuguese-Jewish convert to Christianity under Bilderdijk's influence and was foundational to the Anti-Revolutionary cause in the second quarter of the century through his work as a poet, essayist, lecturer, and author of a multivolume biblical commentary. Groen van Prinsterer (1801–76), Kuyper's mentor, led the Anti-Revolutionary cause after 1848 and was a historian, political theorist, and onetime secretary to King William I.

By pointing to the struggle of past Anti-Revolutionary heroes, Kuyper attempted to give his fellow party members some perspective. Though they faced an election, the very fact that the party had members in the cabinet was a reality that was beyond the dreams of van Prinsterer and his predecessors. Kuyper's interpretation of their successes led him as far as to say that "God the Lord has proved his promise that *there is reward for our labor.*"[31] There had been progress since their movement had formed, especially considering the opposition their representatives faced in the legislative process. Kuyper urged the party, though faced with challenges and defections, to work together for reelection of the cabinet so that they could build on the foundation of the previous years.

Kuyper proceeded to present a path forward. He charged the party to move toward democracy, arguing that it was unacceptable for Christians to maintain the status quo. Though Christians wait for the triumphant return of Christ, they should neither be apathetic nor confined to "reinforcing the dikes." Instead, irrespective of what challenges arise, Christians are to

> position themselves courageously in the breach of this nation and to prepare for *a Christian-democratic development of our national government.* This can still be done *now.* But if you squander this God-given moment and let it pass unused, you will be to blame for having thrown away the future of your country and you will soon bend under the iron fist which will strike you in your Christian liberty and, unsparingly, also in your wallets and property.[32]

Kuyper called his party to be involved in the very center of what he saw as the inevitable forward march of democracy, and he strongly expressed the consequences for the entire nation should this responsibility be neglected. It was imperative that the advancing democracy and state institutions take a Christian shape, or there would be anti-Christian "ochlocracy" (mob rule).

To further motivate his constituency to influence the nation's future direction, Kuyper referred to Israel's collective involvement in selecting a king and to the history of the Calvinist movement in Europe and America. He also pointed to the pivotal place of the "little people" in strengthening governments. In his view, the size

31. Ibid., 216.
32. Ibid., 222.

and demographics of the movement were not a discouragement. The party needed to provide guidance rooted in Christian principles as the country grew more democratic.

Kuyper articulated four aspects that would serve to direct the development of Holland's democracy. First, religion must be held in honor. It is important for authority to be upheld, which requires the presence of conscience. If the government does not honor religion, which benefits the general populace, human nature will regress rather than move forward. Kuyper feared the worst for the nation if religion were ignored and replaced by a strict materialism, for then "a raging fury will turn against the life of our whole society and from the nihilism of despair will arise the triumph of unbridled insanity."[33] Kuyper ultimately hoped that the rule of religion would return to the human heart.

The second aspect was the restoration of freedom of conscience. Kuyper desired a national climate that would allow gospel-rooted belief the "unlimited freedom to develop in accordance with its own genius in the heart of our national life."[34] He had no desire to crush unbelief, only for a playing field that allowed all forms of belief to compete equally in all areas of life.[35]

Third, Holland must be restored in its organic relations. This was not a reactionary stance on social structure that yearned for the return of a pre-nineteenth-century "golden age," which Kuyper actually found to be insufficiently developed by Calvinism. Instead, Kuyper believed the nation could not function in a healthy way unless each part of the entire "national body" participated. Rather than universal suffrage for all individuals, however, Kuyper called for

> *universal* proportional suffrage but on the basis of the *family,* for a restoration of the old guilds in a new form, for Chambers of Labor and Agriculture. Our desire will obtain only when there is next to the

33. Ibid., 224.
34. Ibid.
35. Kuyper says, "Only *this* we do not want: that government arm unbelief to force us, half-armed and handicapped by an assortment of laws, into an unequal struggle with so powerful an enemy. Yet, that *has* happened and is happening *still*. It happens in all areas of popular education, on the higher as well as the lower levels, by means of the power of money, forced examinations, and official hierarchy. For this reason we may never desist from our protest or resistance until the gospel recover its freedom to circulate, until the performance of his Christian duty will again be possible for every Dutch citizen, whether rich or poor" (ibid., 224–25).

political Chamber in the capital also a Chamber of Interests in which all parts of the national body, hence also the church of Jesus Christ, will be represented in fair proportion.[36]

The final aspect was a spirit of compassion poured out over the government. Kuyper viewed the Netherlands as a Christian rather than a pagan nation, and he believed the approach to national anguish should reflect this heritage. In view of the suffering from unemployment, hard labor, and other forms of oppression, Kuyper and his party called for legislation with a heart and officials with sympathy. Labor protection and equal justice for all citizens exemplified the ideal results of such compassion.

Kuyper closed this address by calling for an electoral unity that would preserve the cabinet and by charging the party to "not go limping behind others but run ahead of the procession by the light of prophecy and the radiance of *Maranatha*."[37] The eschatological vision should compel this Calvinist party to attend to its cause with boldness, to continue its charge into public life.[38] Inspired by their predecessors, the Anti-Revolutionaries needed to seize this unique moment in history to influence the direction of their society.

"The Social Question and the Christian Religion"

On November 9–12, 1891, the First Christian Social Congress was held in Amsterdam with over five hundred participants present. As mentioned above, the problem at hand was the social dilemma brought on by industrialization. Many who came to the cities to work in the factories suffered from poor working conditions, long hours, and low wages. The workers were also at the mercy of the "boom and bust" nature of commerce and industry. While a select few grew wealthy from industrialization, this wealth did not reach most of the laborers.[39]

From Kuyper's perspective, the root of the problem lay in the ideas of the French Revolution. This revolt sought to overthrow the power

36. Ibid., 225. For a more detailed discussion of Kuyper's views on suffrage, see Henk E. S. Woldring, "Kuyper's Formal and Comprehension Conceptions of Democracy," in *Kuyper Reconsidered: Aspects of His Life and Work,* ed. Cornelis van der Kooi and Jan de Bruijn (Amsterdam: VU Uitgeverij, 1999), 206–17.

37. Kuyper, "Maranatha," 227.

38. When the election came in the summer, Kuyper's coalition lost.

39. McGoldrick, *Abraham Kuyper,* 73–74.

of the aristocracy and the corrupt church and replace it with the authority of human reason coupled with the autonomy and egoism of the individual.[40] Louis Praamsma describes the fruit of the revolt:

> The result was threefold—a profound social need, a widespread social democratic movement, and a very thorny social problem. The need arose because when people lacked spiritual nourishment, they became eager for material things. The struggle for life became a struggle for money. The wealthy middle class showed the hardness of the human heart in its attitude toward the proletariat, under the cover of the slogan: freedom for everyone. . . . The social democrats pointed out that the *equality* promised by the French revolution had never been realized. They predicted that the oppressed would extort by force what was being taken from them.[41]

Kuyper's speech was set in a social context with a significant class division. A part of this context was the advent of a social democratic movement that correctly identified the social dilemma but had the same human-centered ideological basis as the wealthy liberals. His speech attempted to cultivate a demonstrative compassion rooted in Christian principles, with God restored to the center.

Kuyper began his speech by describing how the social problem had grown out of human misuse of the creation mandate. While the divine ordinances demand that humans develop and provide structure to both nature and society, the reality of sin had resulted in social structures that were far from ideal. Kuyper admitted that human ingenuity and creativity had decisively shaped education and social practice and had brought society beyond barbarism in a general sense, but "although we must concede that such a continuous development of society strengthens belief in a higher providential rule—we cannot for a moment doubt that this intervention, often originating from false principles, has in all ages created unhealthy conditions that could have been healthy. It has in many ways poisoned our mutual relationships and weighed us down with nameless misery."[42] As stated above, Kuyper identified the human-centered ideology of the French Revolution as the

---

40. Praamsma, *Let Christ Be King*, 98.

41. Ibid., 98–99.

42. Abraham Kuyper, *The Problem of Poverty*, ed. James W. Skillen (Grand Rapids: Baker, 1991), 32–33. Skillen's volume is the most recent translation of Kuyper's address to the Christian Social Congress.

false principle that had generated social misery in Holland. For a contrasting principle, Kuyper pointed to Jesus' approach to the poverty of his era.

When speaking of Jesus, Kuyper focused on his compassion and its implications. "Powerful is the trait of compassion, imprinted on every page of the Gospel where Jesus came into contact with the suffering and the oppressed."[43] While he noted that the crucifixion was the ultimate demonstration of Jesus' compassion, Kuyper also informed his audience that Jesus sent the church to influence society through the ministry of the Word, the ministry of charity, and the institution of the equality of brotherhood. Kuyper argued that this Christian influence yielded more tolerable social conditions:

> Earthly welfare no longer weighed heaviest in public estimation; eternal well-being also carried weight. Slavery was snapped at its root and underwent a moral criticism that sapped it as an institution. Men began to be concerned about caring for the poor and for orphans. Accumulation of too much capital was checked by the prohibition of usury. Higher and lower classes approached each other more freely on a more equal footing. The contrast of abundance and scarcity was not erased, but extreme luxury no longer clashed so sharply with dire poverty. Man had not yet arrived at the point where he should be, but at least he was started along a better path; and had the church not gone astray from her simplicity and her heavenly ideal, the influence of the Christian religion on political life and social relationships would eventually have become dominant.[44]

Kuyper cited the conversion of Constantine as the moment when the church's influence began to wane. Indeed, the church became more worldly as a result of imperial sanction. "The salt lost its savor, and social corruption regained its ancient strength—a corruption checked but not brought under control in the lands of the Reformation."[45] While Christ provided the foundation for a better society,

43. Ibid., 38.
44. Ibid., 42.
45. Ibid. This quotation reveals why Kuyper's public theology cannot be saddled with the label "Constantinian." Kuyper made reference to Constantine not to distance himself from the idea that Christians should engage the sociopolitical order but to distinguish his approach to such engagement from that of Constantine. His concern was that the church had become paganized instead of influencing the nations with the salt of Christianity.

his followers' imperfections led to the construction of an unstable social architecture.

What path would lead to the restructuring of society? The social democratic approach would not work because of its faulty principle, so Kuyper provided a Christian alternative. For a better society, "improvement undoubtedly lies—I do not shrink from the word—along a *socialistic* path, provided that you do not mean by 'socialistic' the program of the social democrats, but merely the idea, in itself so beautiful, that our national society is . . . a God-willed *community,* a living, human organism."[46] Specifically, Kuyper outlined seven points that would make up a social program.

The first point was the confession of belief in God as Creator of heaven and earth. Recognition of God's authority and the validity of his ordinances are foundational to the development of any social structure. The second point was that the sphere sovereignty of state and society must be upheld. From Kuyper's perspective, the social question cannot be resolved unless "we respect this duality and thus honor state authority as clearing the way for a free society."[47] Third, as he said in *Maranatha,* Christians must be united in their recognition of society as an organic body. In contrast to individualism, Christians must be mindful that the mystery of human sin and salvation through Christ accord only with a society that is an interconnected whole. Fourth, in contrast to pantheists and pessimists who view the world as determined by some form of fate, Christians must set forth a view of reality rooted in God's providence[48] that encourages Christians to engage in the struggle to change the ills of society and to reinforce the

46. Ibid., 52. Kuyper's positive use of the term *socialistic* should not be construed as an acquiescence to class-based socialism. That was the position of one set of his opponents. Rather, Kuyper used the term to refer to a view of society that was analogous to the description of the church as a "body" in 1 Corinthians 12. He had in mind the idea that society is like a body, a living, interconnected community that considers the welfare of the whole and not just individuals (as in the view of the French Revolution). For Kuyper, the term *socialistic* was useful for conveying the idea that there is a social reality at the center of civilization that is ecclesially based. He said, "We are members of each other, and thus the eye cannot get along without the foot, nor the foot without the eye. It is this human, this scientific, this Christian truth that, because of the French Revolution, people failed to recognize, stoutly denied, and so grievously assailed. Against the individualism of the French Revolution, born from its denial of human community, the whole movement of society in our times is now turning" (ibid., 52).

47. Ibid., 65.

48. In the use of this term, Kuyper was referring to God's direct involvement in the world. Specifically, it was a way to articulate divine sovereignty in relation to the

good. Fifth, Christians should resist attempts to quickly and violently change society. Instead, gradual and lawful change is the best path. Sixth, Christians should acknowledge that all property belongs to God and that all humans are stewards. All humans should exercise responsible use of their goods. Under God, "we have no right of rule except in the context of the organic association of mankind, and thus also in the context of the organic association of its possessions."[49] Seventh, property should not rest in the hands of a privileged few. God's ordinances run counter to the notion of individualistic owner-ship. Kuyper suggested that agrarian regulations should be considerate of all the people in the land.[50]

In addition to these seven points, Kuyper suggested some specific actions. He advocated resistance to legislation that undermined the family, and he urged the exaltation of marriage as an institution. In terms of labor, he argued that a worker should be "able to live as a person created in the image of God."[51] Workers should have the right to a Sabbath and the right to speak up when society is arranged in a way that impedes the possibility of fulfilling the divine calling on their lives.[52] Workers are entitled to fair wages and the possibility of living above subsistence when retirement comes. Kuyper encouraged Christians to speak up as a voice of protest as long as society failed to conform to God's Word. His final words concerning laborers were strong: "To mistreat the workman as a 'piece of machinery' is and remains a violation of his human dignity. Even worse, it is a sin

---

course of history. It was a way to speak of a positive *telos* for the history, which would serve to encourage public engagement rather than withdrawal.

49. Ibid., 67.

50. Ibid., 68. Kuyper was not advocating the nationalization of land, but he was articulating a principle consonant with the idea that "the fruitful field is given by God to *all the people* so that every tribe in Israel might dwell on it and live from it" (68). He was not urging state ownership or even resisting a view of individual possessions. Instead, he was arguing against the kind of individualistic view of land ownership in which there was local authority over landless peasants. Kuyper was critical of the selfish use of such authority. For example, he told a story about Scotland in which fourteen people owned three-fourths of the land. One such person bought a piece of land and expelled the forty-eight families who lived there so it could become a large game preserve. Kuyper proposed that agrarian regulations should prompt those who owned land to recognize their responsibility to the larger human community in a man-ner similar to God's law for Israel.

51. Ibid., 70.

52. Ibid., 70–71.

directly contrary to the sixth commandment: You shall not kill the worker socially."[53]

Kuyper also addressed welfare. First, the government should come to the aid of labor when there are injustices, and labor should be given the right to organize so that it can protect itself. Second, in terms of distributing money to people, Kuyper argued that it should be kept to a minimum, lest it undermine the laborers' work ethic. He preferred that the church attend to almsgiving, stating that "all state relief for the poor is a blot on the honor of your Savior."[54] A final suggestion worthy of note comes from Kuyper's final call for action. He urged Christians to emphasize deeds of love, as the poor cannot merely sit and wait for the reformation of society before receiving any kind of help. The emphasis on deeds revealed Kuyper's desire for concrete action, not merely the recitation of Christian ideals.[55]

What does this speech reveal about Kuyper's public theology? In contrast to the ideals of the French Revolution, the Anti-Revolutionary leader presented an approach to social problems based on confessionally orthodox Christian principles. As seen above, he wanted Christians to propagate and present not only alternative ideas but also alternative practices that would model Christian compassion. Furthermore, this address demonstrated his core desire to move toward a society that operated according to divine ordinances, which in this case meant a respect of sphere sovereignty, the protection of labor, and Christian support of the poor.

"The Blurring of the Boundaries"

In 1892, Kuyper gave the rectorial address at the Free University of Amsterdam. This platform provided him with the opportunity to call attention to what he perceived to be the dominant, and dangerous, worldview at that time: pantheism. From the perspective of Kuyper, pantheism served as the umbrella ideology that encompassed the thought of figures such as Nietzsche, Darwin, Hegel, and Schleiermacher. While it may seem a stretch to group these figures together under one label, James Bratt's comments are instructive:

53. Ibid., 71.
54. Ibid., 78.
55. Ibid., 77.

One might fault Kuyper for the very "blurring of the boundaries" that he criticized in pantheism, but it is more helpful to take the resemblance as a clue to how close Kuyper felt to the forces with which he was wrestling. German Idealism he took to be a marked improvement over the cold rationalism of the eighteenth century, and mystical closure with God more admirable than the calculated ethics of duty. Kuyper's problem was how to harvest the virtues of this impulse without falling into its dechristianizing logic.[56]

Kuyper expressed his concern as follows: "I will not even detain you with an attempt to define this elusive Proteus but will focus on this one point—that pantheism blurs all distinctions, obscures all boundary lines, and shows a tendency to wash out all contrasts."[57] The blurring occurred religiously by reducing the distinction between God and humans, and philosophically by fusing every thesis and antithesis into a synthesis. As a result, all dissimilarities were seen as actually consisting of the same substance. The philosophical aspect posed the greatest danger because it dealt with an image of existing reality over against reality itself. Making specific reference to Kant, Fichte, and Hegel, Kuyper argued that this philosophy "ineluctably takes us out of the really existing world into an abstract world of thought, where it can do what it pleases with the distinctions and antitheses of life."[58]

Why did Kuyper view this as a threat? He feared that this removal of boundaries in logic, spirituality, and religion would yield disastrous consequences, such as the absorption of all legal distinctions into the single idea of the state, the demise of marriage, and a severely weakened, heresy-blind Christianity.[59] Kuyper feared that national and moral death would result from an unchecked pantheism.[60] More specifically, Kuyper saw personal, ecclesiastical, and political consequences of the pantheistic specter.

In terms of personal life, Kuyper argued that character development suffered under the sway of pantheism:

56. Bratt, *Abraham Kuyper,* 363.
57. Abraham Kuyper, "The Blurring of the Boundaries," in *Abraham Kuyper,* 373.
58. Ibid.
59. Ibid., 382–83.
60. Ibid., 387. Kuyper pointed to India and China as examples of nations with a pantheistic worldview. From his perspective, human degradation and an inferior national life are the result of blurring all distinctions.

Only those who relate to God as the holy Friend deepen the features of their own character. . . . No firm character can be formed when the chisel is exchanged for a stub. Character calls for strength of conviction, coupled with an energetic will. It demands a sense of calling, along with the faith that you will succeed therein. Precisely these factors of our personality begin to misfunction when the fixed lines of our life-conception melt and you no longer believe in any familiar truth, in any law governing your will, in any God who calls you and levels all obstacles to that calling. Then the downpours and bubbling seepage reduce the well-graveled roadbed on which you're walking to a giant quagmire in which you stumble and slide. Hence the lament, never more general than in our day, about the lack of character, of impressive personalities, of men with wills of steel. One need not be a devotee of bygone days to be saddened by how flat, unexpressive, and impotent we look compared to the striking figures on Rembrandt's canvases.[61]

Pantheism had yielded a century of leaders with benign convictions at best. There were some great people but few "stars of the first order." Instead, "Second rate imitators have replaced the originals, and at their feet gathers the world weary crowd whose lack of animation their lusterless eye conveys."[62] Social degradation had become commonplace, manifested by the absence of moral absolutes and the rise of crime.[63]

Ecclesiastically, Kuyper lamented the increasing absence of any antithesis between the church and the unregenerate world. In church leadership, particularly the national church, devotees of confessional bounds were ousted, while advocates of doctrinal liberty advanced an agenda of secularization. Unchecked, this could yield a church that served the ends of the state until it was absorbed into the state itself.[64]

Politically, Kuyper argued that the replacement of a belief in a final judgment (which enables one to behold injustice in the world because one's own sense of right can rest in the fact that God will arise to avenge it) with the acceptance of the "pantheistic half-truth that 'the history of the world is the judgment of the world'"[65] would

61. Ibid.
62. Ibid., 389.
63. Ibid., 388–89.
64. Ibid., 390–91.
65. Ibid., 391.

lead to a secularized concept of justice in which legality was nothing other than that created and enforced (and constantly modified) by the government. This malleable notion of right and wrong, rooted in and subject to the whims of a totalitarian state as the instrument of society, displayed a political form of natural selection. Kuyper described the process and the resultant blurred boundary:

> Party succeeds party in gaining the upper hand—Napoleon is replaced by Bourbon, Bourbon by Orleans, Orleans again by Napoleon III, seizing authority by turns because they are temporarily the *stronger*. Rule in the state thus in fact goes to those with *power*, and in this stronger party the right of the stronger celebrates its dubious triumph not only *de facto* but also *in theory*. With that falls the boundary that divides civil authority as the power ordained by God from the people, the society, subordinated by God to that authority. Both are swallowed up in the one all-sufficient state, and that state puts itself in the place of God. The state becomes the highest power and at the same time the source of all right. Government no longer exists because of sin, but the state exists as the ideal of human society, a state before whose apotheosis every knee must bow, by whose grace everyone must live, to whose word everyone must be subject . . . the one all providing state in which all human energy is channeled and seeks to come into its own.[66]

Kuyper feared that the advent of such an expansive state would result in nihilistic anarchy because a power struggle would ensue between an absolutist state (run by a "government of Schleiermacher's virtuosos, that is of academics and geniuses") and the general populace as they sought to gain control over the state. While the elites would argue that power comes from the state, the populace would argue that its demands should be met because it constitutes the state and actually possesses authority. Though the governing faction could exert political control by military means, raw power (which is alone the foundation for order) would eventually lead to devastation for the regnant order when the armies, aware of their power, mounted a coup and taunted the elites with words such as "there are no boundaries, it's all Evolution! What have we done but bring on an inevitable phase in your pantheistic process?"[67] The political result of pantheism would be comparable to a human body when the boundaries have broken

66. Ibid., 392.
67. Ibid., 393.

down between arteries and muscle tissue: inevitable decomposition. The pantheistic, evolutionary process would be fatal.

What alternative did Kuyper offer? In language that initially sounds Anabaptist, Kuyper said that "those who still have faith and discern the danger of blurring the boundaries must start by drawing a line around *their own circle,* must develop *a life of their own* within that circle, must *render account* for the life thus constituted, and so acquire the maturity needed for the struggle they must at some point accept."[68] Kuyper called for a firm boundary between the forces of pantheism and the forces of orthodox Christianity. At this point, Kuyper was calling for a strong public manifestation (which included the development of public institutions such as schools) of the antithesis between what he called the "life-movements" of pantheism and sincere confessional Christian faith. He distinguished his approach from that of the Anabaptists by noting that his approach did not call for self-isolation out of fear of the world. Instead, it was more like a military retreat "behind our defenses so as to improve our weapons and be ready for battle."[69]

In his response to the pantheistic threat, Kuyper called for Christians to develop their own circle on the foundation of palingenesis, God's regeneration and re-creation of both humans and the created order. This principle was to serve as the basis for the unique conviction of Kuyper and his followers, with application to every area of life. Interestingly, he also suggested that other confessional groups, such as Catholics, should develop their own circle and their own institutions. If at least two of these circles formed and produced scholarly development, Kuyper asserted, the pantheist influence could be challenged. He envisioned the result with these words:

> Then, ladies and gentlemen, there *would* be resistance, a spontaneously working force that blessed the entire nation and made itself felt in church, state, and society by virtue of the reality of your conduct and the fact of your existence. To sum it all up: . . . there is only one kind of resistance worth offering, but one that the whole of past history gives the promise of victory. It is this: that you draw a sharp, clear line between the circle of your life and that of *Evolution* and within that circle, awed by the majesty of the Lord, respect every boundary He has established.[70]

68. Ibid., 396.
69. Ibid., 398.
70. Ibid., 401.

If his constituency was willing to draw its own boundary, develop its antithetical life, and engage the social order, then, Kuyper believed, the larger society would stave off the effects of pantheism.

"The Blurring of the Boundaries" reveals Kuyper in a defensive posture, where he responded to threats by asserting his antithetical tendencies. In this speech, he identified and engaged an ideological threat that had sociopolitical ramifications rather than directly addressing specific social ills, as he did at the Christian Social Congress. Though here he posited the development of Christian approaches to public life within confessional circles, he nevertheless had in mind engagement and transformation of the social order. Retrenchment and isolation would be unacceptable and contrary to the turn Kuyper made to public theology in his early ministry and would only cede the development of society more quickly to an all-encompassing state.

The Stone Lectures

In 1898, Kuyper gave the L. P. Stone Lectures at Princeton Theological Seminary. The six lectures, given to an American audience, were the most comprehensive articulation of Kuyper's thought. In them he revealed his public theology by restating and expanding on the themes expressed in his previous speeches. Of particular interest are Kuyper's theological rationale for engaging public life, sphere sovereignty, and the tension between the antithesis and common grace.

Kuyper's objective in the lectures was to set forth Calvinism as a comprehensive life system that provided a Christian perspective and approach to every area of life. He held the opinion that Calvinism most accurately embodied the ideal of Christianity (over against Roman Catholicism and Lutheranism) and stood in contrast to major worldviews such as paganism and Islam.[71] This approach to Calvinism was not strictly a religious system but "an all-embracing system of principles"[72] that provided an approach to every facet of life, including public engagement.

In these lectures, what was Kuyper's theological rationale for public engagement? He argued that common grace (the subject of

71. Abraham Kuyper, *Calvinism: Six Lectures Delivered in the Theological Seminary at Princeton* (New York: Revell, 1899), 13.
72. Ibid., 16.

the next chapter) compels Christians to serve God in every facet of
life. For Kuyper, this nonredemptive grace is given so that believers honor the world and "in every domain, discover the treasures
and develop the potencies hidden by God in nature and in human
life."[73] Public engagement is a responsibility of Christians, and as
they embrace this responsibility, they will discover and develop
systems for domestic, social, and political life that provide alternatives to other worldviews.

In his lecture titled "Calvinism and Politics," Kuyper revisited
the idea of sphere sovereignty that he had articulated at the inauguration of the Free University in 1880. Kuyper's purpose in 1880
was to make a place in society for a Christian university (and for
institutions representative of other worldviews, even if non-Christian). His purpose in 1898 was to demonstrate the broader idea
that Calvinism led to a particular kind of political conception.[74]
In this instance, Kuyper argued for three distinct spheres in the
public realm: state, society, and church.

As Kuyper had stated eighteen years earlier, the root principle
of Calvinism was the sovereignty of God over the entire cosmos,
and the three spheres of state, society, and church derive from
God's primordial sovereignty.[75] Each of these spheres possesses
its own authority within itself. In regard to the state, Kuyper argued that as a result of sin, God instituted ruling authorities for
the purpose of governance. He further suggested that Calvinism
leads to a form of government structured as a republic and that
this was Calvin's preference.[76] Though Kuyper argued that God
ultimately provides this form of public rule, he was adamant that
it was not a theocracy:

> A theocracy was only found in Israel, because in Israel, God intervened immediately. For both by *Urim and Thummim* and by

73. Ibid., 33.
74. As in his speech in 1880 and in "The Blurring of the Boundaries," Kuyper set
his approach to the sociopolitical world in contrast to the radical democracy of the
French Revolution and the all-embracing state rooted in Hegel's philosophy (ibid.,
108–15).
75. Ibid., 99.
76. Peter Heslam argues that Kuyper was disingenuous on this point and states
that Calvin in his *Institutes* (IV.xx.8) showed a distinct preference for aristocracy. See
Peter S. Heslam, *Creating a Christian Worldview: Abraham Kuyper's Lectures on
Calvinism* (Grand Rapids: Eerdmans, 1998), 144.

Prophecy; both by His saving miracles and by His chastising judgments, He held in His own hand the jurisdiction and the leadership
of His people. But the Calvinistic confession of the sovereignty of
God holds good for *all* the world, is true for all nations, and is of
force in all authority, which man exercises over man; even in the
authority which parents possess over their children.[77]

God's sovereignty is mediated through human authority, including
government, and is therefore not the direct rule characteristic of a
theocracy. Moreover, while Kuyper desired government according
to divine ordinances, he had no desire to structure society according to the exact dictates of Mosaic law.

In regard to society, Kuyper argued, God gives sovereignty in
the individual social spheres "in order that it may be sharply and
decidedly expressed that these different developments of social life
have nothing above themselves but God, and that the State cannot
intrude here, and has nothing to command in their domain."[78] The
individual social spheres (such as business, family, educational
institutions, and guilds) have the liberty to function on their own
according to the divine ordinances that God established for each
one. This does not mean that the government can never intervene.
Rather, it becomes involved only when differing spheres clash, when
there is an abuse of weaker individuals within a sphere, or when it
needs to coerce all the spheres to contribute to the maintenance of
the state's natural unity.[79] Above all, the state should protect the
liberty of the various social spheres, allowing them to flourish.

According to Kuyper, the church has a sovereignty within the
state, but not in a Constantinian fashion.[80] Kuyper contended that
Calvinism allows the government to rule apart from the direct influence of the church. While the magistrates are to rule according to
God's divine ordinances, they have independence from the church.
God's Word rules through the conscience of those invested with
governmental authority.[81] In addition, the church allows liberty

77. Kuyper, *Calvinism,* 107–8.
78. Ibid., 116.
79. Ibid., 124.
80. Ibid., 128–29. Kuyper wished to distance himself from Calvin's role in the death
of Servetus, and he contended that the principle that led to this unfortunate incident
lay in Constantinianism, not in the essential principles of Calvinism.
81. Ibid., 133–35.

of conscience, speech, and worship in society, though individuals within local churches are subject to the judgment of the clergy.[82]

Kuyper's expression of sphere sovereignty in the Stone Lectures set forth a view of a pluralistic society in which God's sovereignty was differentiated throughout three major spheres (though there are many smaller individual spheres in society) that respect one another's boundaries. In this view, the Calvinistic principle yielded a nontheocratic, republican society that promoted the development of the created order when the spheres operated as God intended.

Where did the antithesis and common grace come into tension?[83] Kuyper's lectures on science and art revealed this tension without adequate resolution, but the lectures continue to suggest avenues of public engagement for Christians. In the lecture "Calvinism and Science," Kuyper first argued that common grace leads to a love for science and that it gives science its own academic domain, but he then made a stark contrast between two kinds of science.[84] There were those he called Normalists, who look only at natural data, and there were Abnormalists, who look at the natural realm but find their ideal norm in the Triune God. The ultimate difference between the two was *"two kinds of human consciousness*: that of the regenerate and the unregenerate."[85] In effect, this meant that Christians and non-Christians have different *kinds* of minds, and as a result, they perceive the entire universe differently and develop approaches to science that reflect their perspectives. Kuyper did not argue that only one group should do science but that each should be allowed to pursue the discipline in its own circle.[86] In this lecture, the antithesis was set forth as fact to be acknowledged by Christians and others in society.

82. Ibid., 138–41. Kuyper went on to argue that it was the "Calvinistic Netherlands" (Kuyper's term) that promoted freedom of thought and expression throughout society, even if there was a state church. He said, "Whosoever was elsewhere straightened, could first enjoy the liberty of ideas and the liberty of press, on Calvinistic ground" (ibid., 141).

83. For a study of antithesis and common grace in the Dutch Calvinist tradition, see Jacob Klapwijk, "Antithesis and Common Grace," in *Bringing into Captivity Every Thought: Capita Selecta in the History of Christian Evaluations of Non-Christian Philosophy*, ed. Jacob Klapwijk, Sander Griffioen, and Gerben Groenewoud (Lanham, Md.: University Press of America, 1991), 169–90.

84. Kuyper, *Calvinism*, 155–72.

85. Ibid., 183.

86. Ibid., 184.

In the lecture "Calvinism and Art," Kuyper argued that common grace enables the production of art and inspires Christians and non-Christians alike.[87] Rather than contending for a particularly Christian conception of art, Kuyper asserted that "Calvinism, on the contrary, has taught us that all liberal arts are gifts that God imparts promiscuously to believers and unbelievers, yea, that, as history shows, these gifts have flourished even in a larger measure outside the holy circle."[88] Art is truly "commonly" produced. Furthermore, while a part of Kuyper's objective in this lecture was to argue that Calvinism had emancipated art from the church (particularly the Roman Church), he also wished to assert and promote the view that the world of art (painting, music, and poetry) should develop to its fullest in its expression of all of life.[89] This development could be achieved by Christians or non-Christians. The important point was that the realm of art, whether related to the church or not, should enjoy the support of Christians.

Kuyper's argument for art was in direct contrast to his perspective on science, as Peter Heslam observes:

> That Kuyper was able to display a positive approach to the arts was largely due to his doctrine of common grace, which in this lecture, in contrast to his lecture on science, is emphasized at the expense of his doctrine of the antithesis, which plays no significant role. This discrepancy is one of the clearest indications of what is perhaps the central tension in Kuyper's thought between the antithesis and corresponding isolation on the one hand, and common grace and corresponding engagement and accommodation on the other.[90]

In the Stone Lectures, Kuyper left this tension unresolved, but he did achieve his objective of finding ways to encourage Christian engagement of the sciences and patronage of the arts.

Kuyper's lectures at Princeton displayed the basis for his public theology (common grace), an approach to society under God's sovereignty, and the central tension in his thought between antithesis and common grace. His version of Calvinism not only promoted but also prompted Christian public engagement in all areas of life.

87. Ibid., 217.
88. Ibid., 216.
89. Ibid., 221.
90. Heslam, *Creating a Christian Worldview,* 222.

In certain arenas, this engagement was to take place in a Christian circle, while in others, it was to take place in the midst of society in general. Either way, he called Christians to recognize and accept their responsibility to discover God's ordinances and to develop the potentialities of creation.

The Prime Minister of the Netherlands: 1901–5

The national parliamentary election of 1901 gave the Anti-Revolutionary Party and the Roman Catholic Party forty-nine seats in Parliament. In addition, the Free Anti-Revolutionaries (a more aristocratic group that split from Kuyper's party over the issue of expanding suffrage) won seven seats. This gave the coalition of confessional parties a majority, and Queen Wilhelmina appointed Abraham Kuyper prime minister of the Netherlands.[91] This marked the apex of his career. What does this period of national prominence reveal about Kuyper's public theology?

One of the most significant aspects of Kuyper's public theology is reflected in the coalition that made possible his ascendence to this high public office. While Kuyper made clear that there were funda-mental confessional differences between Catholics and Protestants, as early as 1879 he also acknowledged that there were principles around which they could unite, such as a commitment to confes-sional education.[92] The coalition demonstrated that Kuyper did not demand a rigid precision in religious worldviews as a prerequisite to political alliance. Moreover, it demonstrated that there are states of affairs that can be recognized and agreed on by, at the very least, confessional groups that have deep differences.

In Kuyper's approach to governance, his intent was to lead the government toward a genuine pluralism, which, from his perspective, meant the inclusion of the Christian part of the population.[93] The pri-mary issue in this regard was education, and Kuyper sought equality of status and support for private schools.[94] In addition, Kuyper sought to govern according to divine ordinances, though he did not desire to create a theocracy or a "clerical" government, as his detractors averred.

91. Langley, *Practice of Political Spirituality,* 72. Also see McGoldrick, *Abraham Kuyper,* 186–89.
92. McGoldrick, *Abraham Kuyper,* 190–91.
93. Ibid., 199.
94. Ibid., 199–200.

The law of God was intended to be a foundation, while, according to Kuyper, civil government was a medium or agent of common grace. The recognition of this fact did two things. First, as noted in the Stone Lectures, it made Christian engagement in culture and politics a possibility and a responsibility. Second, in this particular context, it implied that Christians, who were a minority, were to function as leaven in society for the benefit of the entire society rather than attempt to construct either a theocracy or Dutch Constantinianism.[95]

In matters of legislation, Kuyper sought to help those who were exploited by employers; to assist the poor, ill, and elderly; to promote greater morality; to elevate the social status of the *kleine luyden;* and to resolve the education issue. While Kuyper succeeded in passing measures such as a revised liquor license law, and while his approach to the great railroad strike of 1903 highlighted a clash between Christian and socialist worldviews (Christians viewed law through the lens of revelation, while their opponents ignored it),[96] Kuyper's most significant achievement may have been the Higher Education Act passed in May 1905. With this law, Christian higher education gained equal status with humanist education in state universities. Though at the time the law affected only the Vrije Universiteit as an institution, it also enabled churches and private organizations to create special professorial chairs at state universities, thus enabling more Christian influence in secular establishments.[97] This law made it possible for Kuyper's constituency to be educated on the same level as others in society and heightened the possibility for Christians to enter places of social influence. It amounted to a kind of Christian emancipation.[98]

Kuyper's tenure as prime minister ended in 1905. He remained prominent until his death in 1920, but he did not have the same scope of influence in Dutch life. As prime minister he attempted to put his public theology into practice by seeking to govern according to divine ordinances while permitting worldview pluralism in society. His tenure may not have been the most successful (this could be as much a result of his personality as his political approach),[99] but it

95. Ibid., 205.

96. Langley, *Practice of Political Spirituality,* 100. Also see McGoldrick, *Abraham Kuyper,* 199–204.

97. McGoldrick, *Abraham Kuyper,* 204–5.

98. Langley, *Practice of Political Spirituality,* 86.

99. McGoldrick, *Abraham Kuyper,* 207.

is evident that he sought to govern in a manner commensurate with
his theology.

AN ANALYSIS OF KUYPER'S PUBLIC THEOLOGY

Now that we have a snapshot of Kuyper's public theology during
his zenith, the next task is to evaluate it. In particular, what kind of
public theology was it? Was it confessional, apologetic, a hybrid, or
something different?

It is not insignificant that the survey of Kuyper's public theology
consisted primarily of various forms of public address. Though
Kuyper was a prolific author, he best set forth his public theology
in public addresses. In the public forum, Kuyper presented a public
theology that contained elements of confessional and apologetic public theology, but he primarily achieved his intended effect through
rhetorical power. His arguments were set forth in rhetoric that
moved his audience to action. Before making the case that Kuyper
was a rhetorical public theologian, this section needs to address the
relationship between Kuyper and the approaches to public theology
presented in chapter 1.

Kuyper's affinities to the public theologies of the apologetically
inclined Max Stackhouse and the confessionally inclined Ronald
Thiemann are significant. Kuyper's focus on common grace, recognition of horizontal pluralism in civil society, eschatological emphasis,
and search for the ordinances of creation are apologetic elements he
has in common with Stackhouse. More specifically, Kuyper's views
overlap with all nine of Stackhouse's themes, though Kuyper did not
use the same language. For example, Stackhouse promotes the theme
of liberation using language that speaks of social change, especially
in terms of rectifying patterns of oppression. Kuyper's entire public
project can be construed as a liberation mission for the *kleine luyden,*
who were relegated to the margins of society. In addition, Stackhouse's
theme of moral law bears resemblance to Kuyper's search for divine
ordinances, and the theme of ecclesiology fits Kuyper's desire for
worldview pluralism in society. Regarding warrants for his public
theology, Kuyper, while not making reference to the Wesleyan quadrilateral, utilized Scripture, tradition, and reason, though not in the
exact way Stackhouse does.

With his focus on antithesis, Kuyper, like Thiemann, desired to find a way to maintain the integrity of Christian confession while participating in public life. Thiemann's characteristics, which reaffirm the public role of religion and the desire for religious convictions and theological analysis to affect the structure of public life and policy, find resonance in Kuyper's "Sphere Sovereignty" and "The Social Question and the Christian Religion." A final comparison is noteworthy. While Kuyper was creative in crafting neo-Calvinism in a way that served his public aims (a view shared by scholars sympathetic and critical), unlike Thiemann, he would not suggest a potentially radical alteration of the Christian tradition in the search for effective public engagement.

While these apologetic and confessional aspects are significant elements of Kuyper's public theology, it can best be characterized by what caused its greatest influence: rhetoric.

John Bolt suggests that it may be best to perceive Kuyper as a poet. By highlighting his rhetorical and mythopoetic perspective rather than merely focusing on his theological and philosophical ideas, one arrives at a view of Kuyper's public theology that helps to explain his public effectiveness.[100] Bolt argues:

> To understand Kuyper's success as a *movement* leader, emancipating and prodding into action the marginalized Dutch orthodox *Gereformeerde kleine luyden,* we must see him reviving and using a Dutch, Christian-historical imagination through powerful rhetoric, well-chosen biblical images and national mythology. That is what I mean by Kuyper as "poet," a man of *rhetoric* and *mythos* more than a man of *logos* and *wetenschap.* Here we find a unity to Kuyper's multifaceted career as churchman, theologian, journalist, politician. Kuyper knew triumphant political technique was not enough, politics alone cannot save the world. What then? Few have stated it better in our era than Alexander Solzhenitsyn, who learned it from Dostoyevsky: "Beauty will save the world." That is, it is art, the historical mythology imaginatively captured in a people's literature, paintings and festivals, the iconographic emblems; it is these that stir hearts and mobilize hands to change the world. Good art nourishes our capacity for self-tran-

---

100. For a detailed view of this, see John Bolt, *A Free Church, a Holy Nation: Abraham Kuyper's American Public Theology* (Grand Rapids: Eerdmans, 2001), 3–79. An abbreviated summary of this chapter can be found in John Bolt, "Abraham Kuyper as Poet: Another Look at Kuyper's Critique of the Enlightenment," in *Kuyper Reconsidered,* 30–41.

scendence, and is our only access to other people's experience, including that past. Literature is "the living memory of a nation . . . [that], together with language, preserves and protects a nation's soul."[101]

In what ways did Kuyper the artist stir hearts and mobilize hands? One way he did this was by invoking the names William Bilderdijk and Isaac da Costa, as mentioned earlier. By reference to these two figures, Kuyper invoked the national spirit in his people. Further, Kuyper tied biblical images to national history, as when he launched *De Standaard* and invoked a day of Dutch liberation.[102]

Bolt also notes how, at an 1897 celebration of twenty-five years of *De Standaard*, Herman Bavinck in public compared Dutch poets and statesmen and gave Kuyper the literary edge over the poets Bilderdijk and da Costa. In addition, Bolt points to James Bratt's comparison of Kuyper and Martin Luther King Jr. Both King and Kuyper were authors but were regarded best as orators. Both men also utilized the imagery from national history to rouse their constituency and advance their cause.[103]

Kuyper's rhetorical approach is also revealed in Jan de Bruijn's article "Abraham Kuyper as a Romantic." In this article, two aspects of romanticism are worthy of note. First, there is the tendency to think in terms of opposites. Kuyper often used this approach when articulating the validity of the Christian position over against another worldview or political system, from pantheism to socialism to the French Revolution. A second key aspect of Kuyper's romanticism was his "predilection for the dramatic moment, for poses and theatricality . . . used like brilliant actors."[104] This element can be clearly seen in some of Kuyper's speeches, such as the closing words of "Sphere Sovereignty," "Maranatha," or "The Blurring of the Boundaries." The use of the dramatic moment served Kuyper's rhetoric well. In

101. Bolt, "Abraham Kuyper as Poet," 34–35.
102. Ibid., 38. "Kuyper knew what he was doing when on the 'day of Dutch liberation, a day that represented the breakthrough of the Calvinist spirit,' his lead editorial alluded to William of Orange, the Sea Beggars, the Dutch national spirit, and the glory of God, followed by a jeremiad about the nation's departure from God's ordinances. After a word of encouragement to the small 'Gideon's band' to continue in battle, Kuyper concluded with a prayer that the God of history might use the commemorative occasion to renew the Dutch nation" (38).
103. Ibid., 40.
104. Jan de Bruijn, "Abraham Kuyper as a Romantic," in *Kuyper Reconsidered*, 43.

the following description of Kuyper, de Bruijn reveals the potency of Kuyper as a romantic rhetorician:

> Kuyper was a man of many qualities. His personality was masterful, his knowledge exceptionally wide-ranging; he was a skillful teacher and polemicist; his energy was tireless and he was a brilliant organizer and a tactical genius. Last but not least, with his baroque eloquence with which he repeatedly urged his followers on, he turned the middle classes into a political force, thus radically altering the political balance of power in Holland. It is no wonder that his supporters revered him as a prophet, as a leader sent by God, as the "Lord's anointed" who like a second Moses had led them to the Promised Land. Kuyper, too, saw himself in this light and as a romantic he could make good use of historical and biblical imagery, symbols and myths to emphasize the special and sacred nature of his struggle and leadership.[105]

Of all the qualities listed, it was Kuyper's eloquence and rhetorical use of imagery that made him such a forceful public influence. Like Bolt, de Bruijn suggests that Kuyper's use of artistry provided the greatest force in mobilizing the *kleine luyden*.

While Kuyper's public theology was rhetorical, this does not mean that convictions did not lie beneath his exceptional public artistry. An idea such as sphere sovereignty, for example, was not a mere instrument employed in the service of Kuyper's ambition. Rather, Kuyper utilized his mythopoetic imagination to persuade the public of his theological and philosophical positions. Kuyper maintained the view that there were divine ordinances that could be discovered and set forth as a guide for society, and his goal was not merely to amaze audiences with poetic language but to prompt them to public engagement, a goal he accomplished. In addition, one cannot neglect Kuyper's emphasis on common grace and antithesis[106] as the chief rationales for forms of participation in public life. In articulating

105. Ibid., 50.
106. Interestingly, de Bruijn notes that Kuyper was a divided personality, which could help explain why common grace and antithesis were never fully resolved. He says, "For like every romantic, Kuyper was not a unified personality; he was no simple one-dimensional figure, but possessed an extremely complex character structure, composed of different layers and often contradictory tendencies, wishes and emotions. In many respects he was a divided and tormented person whose life was not easy and who suffered periods of deep depression. However, he survived because of a faith that expressed itself on the one hand in mystical longings, and on the other in an unremitting, almost compulsive activity and struggle to realize his religious ideals"

these opposing tendencies, Kuyper gave as much place to argument as to rhetoric (as seen in the Stone Lectures).

This chapter presented a snapshot of Kuyper's public theology, revealing that he utilized artistically clothed arguments to achieve goals made possible by the reality of common grace. The next chapter considers the theology of common grace and its relationship with pneumatology.

(ibid., 45). An interesting question is, Was Kuyper's primary concern the practical achievement of his goals rather than the precise articulation of a theological construct to undergird his mission?

3

THE SPIRIT OF KUYPER'S PUBLIC
THEOLOGY

The previous chapter revealed that common grace was Abraham Kuyper's theological rationale for public engagement.[1] This chapter examines this theological rationale in more detail and reveals the implicit relationship between common grace and Kuyper's doctrine of the Holy Spirit's work in creation.

1. Abraham Kuyper's doctrine of common grace has been summarized in several books and articles. See Peter S. Heslam, *Creating a Christian Worldview: Abraham Kuyper's Lectures on Calvinism* (Grand Rapids: Eerdmans, 1998), 117–23; Jacob Klapwijk, "Antithesis and Common Grace," in *Bringing into Captivity Every Thought: Capita Selecta in the History of Christian Evaluations of Non-Christian Philosophy,* ed. Jacob Klapwijk, Sander Griffioen, and Gerben Groenewoud (Lanham, Md.: University Press of America, 1991), 170–79; Wayne A. Kobes, "Sphere Sovereignty and the University: Theological Foundations of Abraham Kuyper's View of the University and Its Role in Society" (Ph.D. diss., Florida State University, 1993), 122–49; James E. McGoldrick, *Abraham Kuyper: God's Renaissance Man* (Auburn, Mass.: Evangelical Press, 2000), 141–57; Louis Praamsma, *Let Christ Be King: Reflections on the Life and Times of Abraham Kuyper* (Jordan Station, Ont.: Paideia, 1985), 139–44; Cornelius Van Til, *Common Grace and the Gospel* (Phillipsburg, N.J.: Presbyterian & Reformed, 1972), 14–22; Henry R. Van Til, *The Calvinistic Concept of Culture,* 3rd ed. (Philadelphia: Presbyterian & Reformed, 2001), 117–36; and S. U. Zuidema, "Common Grace and Christian Action in Abraham Kuyper," in *Communication and Confrontation,* ed. Gerben Groenewoud, trans. Harry Van Dyke (Toronto: Wedge, 1972), 52–105.

Kuyper's opponents labeled his theology "neo-Calvinism," a title intended to distinguish Kuyper's work from that of John Calvin.[2] While Kuyper did seek to develop the Calvinist principle more fully and did so creatively, his development of this doctrinal heritage was not a complete innovation. Regarding the doctrine of common grace, Kuyper's work was clearly rooted in, related to, and an expansion of the work of Calvin.

ABRAHAM KUYPER, THE NEO-CALVINIST ON COMMON GRACE

Calvin on Common Grace in Brief

To demonstrate that Kuyper's doctrine of common grace was not a pure innovation and departure from John Calvin, we need to show that Calvin himself taught this doctrine. Herman Kuiper's *Calvin on Common Grace* will be our guide. Kuiper's book exhaustively surveys Calvin's *Institutes of the Christian Religion* and his biblical commentaries and reveals the explicit and implicit presence of this doctrine. What follows is a sample of the evidence, selected to illustrate the three major aspects of common grace: (1) God is merciful and beneficent toward all of humanity in the provision of life and various blessings; (2) all humans have a capacity for morality that manifests itself in acts of justice and virtue; and (3) because humans have the ability to reason and understand, the study of nature and history, persons and societies is possible and useful to believers and nonbelievers alike. In the first place, it is important to point out that Calvin did not actually use the term *common grace,* but he did speak of a grace that is nonsalvific and given to the entire creation.[3] Kuiper classifies these forms of grace as universal, which extends to the entire biophysical order; general, which extends to all human beings; and covenantal, which extends to elect and nonelect members of the covenant community. For the scope of the present work, the first two classifications are directly relevant.

2. See John Bolt, *A Free Church, a Holy Nation: Abraham Kuyper's American Public Theology* (Grand Rapids: Eerdmans, 2001), 443–64. See also Cornelis Pronk, "Neo-Calvinism," *Reformed Theological Journal* 11 (1995): 42–56.

3. Herman Kuiper, *Calvin on Common Grace* (Grand Rapids: Smitter Book Company, 1928), 177.

Kuiper states that universal common grace is not extensively taught in Calvin's works, but it is present. In Calvin's *Institutes,* an example can be found in the third book, chapter 2:

> Nor does it make any difference that, while the wicked are plied with the huge and repeated benefits of God's bounty, they bring upon themselves a heavier judgment. For they neither think nor recognize that these benefits come to them from the Lord's hand; or if they do recognize it, they do not within themselves ponder his goodness. Hence, they cannot be apprised of his mercy any more than brute animals can, which, according to their condition, receive the same fruit of God's liberality, yet perceive it not.[4]

While the term *grace* is not used, Kuiper interprets the language of divine mercy and liberality to be synonymous with it. This passage reveals that Calvin saw God as gracious to the biophysical order (humans and animals, in particular) by virtue of an unmerited generosity.

Kuiper also points to the commentaries, where, for example, Calvin used the term *universal grace* in the following comment on Isaiah 44:3: "But these words of the prophet have a wider signification, because he does not speak merely of the Spirit of regeneration, but alludes to the universal grace which is spread over all the creatures."[5] This reference reveals that Calvin held to the doctrine of a universal common grace. These two examples are sufficient to demonstrate that Kuiper does not make an unfounded claim.

While Kuiper admits that Calvin's works contain minimal references to universal common grace, concerning general common grace he says:

> It strikes us how often and how emphatically Calvin assures us that there is a divine grace which touches mankind in general and every individual member of the human race in particular. Calvin never seems to grow weary of telling us that God is beneficent to humankind; that God manifests paternal clemency toward men in general and bestows many excellent blessings upon them; that God loves the human race and shows concern for its welfare.[6]

4. John Calvin, *Institutes of the Christian Religion,* ed. John T. McNeill, trans. Ford Lewis Battles (Philadelphia: Westminster, 1960), III.ii.32.
5. John Calvin, *Commentary on the Book of the Prophet Isaiah,* vol. 3, trans. William Pringle (Grand Rapids: Baker, 1979), 360.
6. Kuiper, *Calvin on Common Grace,* 82.

Kuiper proceeds to present an expansive list of references to general common grace found in the *Institutes* and Calvin's commentaries. For the purposes of this work, two selections from each will suffice.

The fifth chapter of the first book of the *Institutes* contains the following:

> Certain philosophers, accordingly, long ago not ineptly called man a microcosm because he is a rare example of God's power, goodness, and wisdom, and contains within himself enough miracles to occupy our minds, if only we are not irked at paying attention to them. Paul, having stated that the blind can find God by feeling after him, immediately adds that he ought not to be sought afar off [Acts 17:27]. For each one undoubtedly feels within the heavenly grace that quickens him.[7]

Here the term *grace* is used to speak of the fact that humans are kept alive from moment to moment. This fits with the facet of common grace that speaks of God's preservation of life.

An especially noteworthy passage is found in the third chapter of the second book:

> In every age there have been persons who, guided by nature, have striven toward virtue throughout life. I have nothing to say against them even if many lapses can be noted in their moral conduct. For they have by the very zeal of their honesty given proof that there was some purity in their nature. . . . These examples, accordingly, seem to warn us against adjudging man's nature wholly corrupted, because some men have by its prompting not only excelled in remarkable deeds, but conducted themselves most honorably throughout life. But here it ought to occur to us that amid this corruption of nature there is some place for God's grace; not such grace as to cleanse it, but to restrain it inwardly. . . . In his elect the Lord cures these diseases in a way we shall soon explain. Others he merely restrains by throwing a bridle over them only that they may not break loose, inasmuch as he foresees their control to be expedient to preserve all that is. Hence some are restrained by shame from breaking out into many kinds of foulness, others by the fear of the law—even though they do not, for the most part, hide their impurity. Still others, because they consider an honest manner of life profitable, in some measure aspire to it. Others rise above the common lot, in order by their excellence to keep the rest obedient to them. Thus God by his providence bridles

7. Calvin, *Institutes,* I.v.3.

perversity of nature, that it may not break forth into action; but he does not purge it within.[8]

In this passage, Calvin uses the term *grace* to speak of the restraint of sin among the human race. This restraint takes place in a variety of ways, from inward disposition to the presence of law. These forms of restraint are also evidence of a capacity for morality and an ability to perform acts of justice and virtue. This emphasis in particular reveals an approach to general common grace that finds further development in Abraham Kuyper.

Kuiper's examination of Calvin's commentaries reveals Calvin's use of the term *general grace* in his reflection on the phrase "O God, the God of the spirits of all flesh" in Numbers 14:22:

> There is no question but that Moses applies this epithet to God in connexion with the present matter; as if he desired to induce God to preserve His own work, just as a potter spares the vessels formed by himself. To the same effect is the prayer of Isaiah: "But now, O Lord, thou art our father; we are the clay, and thou our potter; and we are all the work of thy hand. Be not wroth very sore" (Isa. lxiv. 8, 9), for hence he alleges a reason why God should relent, and be inclined to mercy. There is this difference, that Isaiah refers to that special grace wherewith God had embraced His people, whereas Moses carries his address further, viz., to the general grace of creation. It is of little importance whether we choose to expound this with reference to all animals, or only to the human race, since Moses merely prays that, since God is the Creator and Maker of the world, He should not destroy the men whom He has formed, but rather have pity upon them, as being His work.[9]

In this passage, the term *grace* refers to the preservation of all life.

Another significant passage is found in Calvin's commentary on John's Gospel. In regard to John 1:9, Calvin interprets the phrase about the light "which enlighteneth every man" as follows:

> From this *light* the rays are diffused over all mankind, as I have already said. For we know that men have this peculiar excellence which raises

---

8. Ibid., II.iii.3.

9. John Calvin, *Commentaries on the Four Last Books of Moses Arranged in the Form of Harmony*, vol. 3, trans. Charles William Bingham (Grand Rapids: Baker, 1979), 112–13. See also Calvin's comments on Acts 17:25–29 for reference to how God is bestowing preserving grace on human life.

them above other animals, that they are endued with reason and intelligence, and that they carry the distinction between right and wrong
engraven on their conscience. There is no man, therefore, whom some
perception of the eternal *light* does not reach.[10]

Here Calvin describes the effects of general common grace, manifested not only as the restraint of sin by means of human conscience
but also as provision of reason and intelligence, which speaks to the
issues of moral capacity and the possibility of the study of nature,
history, and society with benefits for all.[11]

The examples given above, while not exhaustive, demonstrate that
common grace is not a doctrine that originated in the Netherlands
in the late nineteenth century. At the very least, Calvin held the view
that a divine grace is given to the biophysical order that restrains sin,
sustains life, and provides specific gifts to humans.[12]

The focus now turns to Abraham Kuyper, who developed the
doctrine of common grace beyond Calvin, though not in a manner
that departed from biblical and Reformational bases.

Abraham Kuyper on Common Grace, the Key to Public Theology

Kuyper articulated his doctrine of common grace in the Stone
Lectures and in his three-volume treatment *De Gemeene Gratie*
(Common Grace), written as a series of articles for *De Heraut* (The
Herald) from 1895 to 1901. Kuyper described common grace, as
distinct from particular grace, as follows:

> This manifestation of grace served ultimately not to save us but to
> bring out the glory of the Divine Being, and only in the second place,
> as a consequence of this end, to snatch us from our self-sought ruin.
> This manifestation of grace consisted in restraining, blocking, or re-

10. John Calvin, *Commentary on the Gospel according to John,* trans. William
Pringle (Grand Rapids: Baker, 1979), 38.

11. Kuiper points out that it is a significant part of general common grace that
humans were not created as animals and that God has given the light of intelligence to
humans, particularly after the fall (Kuiper, *Calvin on Common Grace,* 182–85).

12. This is not a unique conclusion. For example, see Heslam, *Creating a Christian
Worldview,* 177–78; William Masselink, *General Revelation and Common Grace: A
Defense of the Historic Reformed Faith* (Grand Rapids: Eerdmans, 1953), 187; Mc-
Goldrick, *Abraham Kuyper,* 152–54; and Zuidema, "Common Grace and Christian
Action in Abraham Kuyper," 53.

directing the consequences that would otherwise have resulted from sin. It intercepts the natural outworking of the poison of sin and either diverts and alters it or opposes and destroys it. For that reason we must distinguish two dimensions in this manifestation of grace: 1. a *saving* grace, which in the end abolishes sin and completely undoes its consequences; and 2. a *temporal restraining* grace, which holds back and blocks the effect of sin. The former, that is saving grace, is in the nature of the case *special* and restricted to the elect. The second, *common* grace, is extended to the whole of our human life.[13]

Kuyper articulated the same idea with a slightly different nuance in the Stone Lectures:

In this also, placing itself before the face of God, it [Calvinism] has not only honored *man* for the sake of his likeness to the Divine image, but also *the world* as a Divine creation, and has at once placed to the front the great principle that there is a *particular grace* which works Salvation, and also a *common grace* by which God, maintaining the life of the world, relaxes the curse which rests upon it, arrests its process of corruption, and thus allows the untrammelled development of our life in which to glorify Himself as Creator.[14]

In both of these definitive statements on common grace, Kuyper was concerned to show a clear distinction between a grace directed exclusively toward the elect and another that extends to the entire creation. Common to both descriptions is language about the restraint of sin or the relaxation of the complete effects of the fall into sin. This language of restraint and relaxation expresses the recognition that, while the world has been altered and even distorted because of sin, it is not "lost" in the sense that Christians must escape from rather than engage in the created order and hence the public realm. The description in the Stone Lectures, given in a context of lauding Calvinism over against other worldviews, adds an emphasis concerning development of life, a central factor in Kuyper's public theology.

In making the distinction between special and common grace, Kuyper did not intend to give the perception that there is no rela-

13. Abraham Kuyper, "Common Grace," in *Abraham Kuyper: A Centennial Reader,* ed. James D. Bratt (Grand Rapids: Eerdmans, 1998), 167–68. The translation is by John Vriend.

14. Abraham Kuyper, *Calvinism: Six Lectures Delivered in the Theological Seminary at Princeton* (New York: Revell, 1899), 30–31.

tionship between the two. Rather, he argued that common grace serves as a condition for special grace by making it possible for the elect to be born, a significant point in light of the centrality of election to Kuyper's entire theological enterprise.[15] Though sin entered the world, the fall did not yield the consequences of the curse in an unbridled manner. According to Kuyper, in the "non-arrival of what was prophesied for ill we see the emergence of a saving and long-suffering grace."[16] This grace of creation was made possible by Christ as the mediator of creation, the eternal Word.[17] Kuyper called Christ the root of common grace by virtue of this activity.[18] If there were no common grace, creation would have been destroyed, or at the very least, the conditions for life would have been so horrific that "the church of God would not have had a place to strike root anywhere. . . . It would be massacred in less than no time."[19] Common grace has a constant aspect that not only sustains life but also makes possible a "good" life.

15. For the centrality of election in Kuyper's theology, see Willem van der Schee, "Kuyper's Archimedes' Point: The Reverend Abraham Kuyper on Election," in *Kuyper Reconsidered: Aspects of His Life and Work,* ed. Cornelis van der Kooi and Jan de Bruijn (Amsterdam: VU Uitgeverij, 1999), 102–10.

16. Kuyper, "Common Grace," 167.

17. Kuyper distinguishes between Christ the eternal Word as the mediator of creation and Jesus Christ the incarnate Word as the mediator of redemption. The following comments are of interest: "Holy Scripture repeatedly tells us of the intertwinement of the life of special grace with that of common grace but simultaneously discloses that the point at which the two come together is not Christ's birth in Bethlehem but his eternal existence as the *Eternal Word*" (ibid., 183). "He is not enlisted *by* the Decree and *for* the execution of that Decree, but that Decree is *His*. In what people call the 'eternal counsel of peace' He incorporates himself in that Decree and obligates himself to bring about its fulfillment. But just as truly as He obligates himself in the decree of redemption to be the Mediator of sinners, so in the same decree He is the Mediator of creation. Not first the Mediator of redemption and now, to achieve that role, also admitted as Mediator of creation. But rather, first the original Mediator of creation and after that also the Mediator of redemption to make possible the enforcement and fulfillment of the decree of creation and everything entailed in it" (ibid., 185). "Therefore common grace must have a formative impact on special grace and vice versa. All separation of the two must be vigorously opposed. Temporal and eternal life, our life in the world and our life in the church, religion and civil life, church and state, and so much more must go hand in hand. They may not be separated. To avoid such separation we must consistently make a sharp distinction between them, for it is on the correctness of this *distinction* that the progress of life depends" (ibid., 185–86).

18. Ibid., 186. Though he used this language, Kuyper's work implies that the Spirit is also central to common grace, as will be demonstrated below.

19. Ibid., 169.

Kuyper was also concerned to articulate the proper relationship between nature and grace. In this regard, a problem occurs when grace is distinguished from nature, rendering the significance of Christ exclusive to the spiritual realm. Kuyper described the dilemma:

> People fall into one-sidedness in the opposite direction if, reflecting on the Christ, they think exclusively of the blood shed in atonement and refuse to take account of the significance of Christ for the body, for the visible world, and for the outcome of world history. Consider carefully: by taking this tack you run the danger of isolating Christ for your soul and you view life in and for the world as something that exists *alongside* your Christian religion, not controlled by it. Then the word "Christian" seems appropriate to you only when it concerns certain matters of faith or things directly connected with the faith—your church, your school, missions and the like—but all the remaining spheres of life fall for you *outside the Christ*. In the world you conduct yourself as others do; that is less holy, almost unholy, territory which must somehow take care of itself. You only have to take a small step more before landing in the Anabaptist position which concentrated all sanctity in the human soul and dug a deep chasm between this inward-looking spirituality and life all around.[20]

If the Christian life is confined to the soul, Kuyper argued, then the rest of life is separated from any kind of grace, and ordinary life becomes unholy. To the contrary, Kuyper asserted that Christ, who created the world, is connected to nature by virtue of the Creator/creation relationship and to grace by virtue of his role as redeemer and ultimately re-creator of the world.[21] In making this connection, Kuyper aimed to demonstrate that the biophysical order is not set against grace in a mutually exclusive fashion. If grace and nature are not radically separate, then it is possible to speak of common grace.

How did Kuyper describe the common grace/nature relationship? Instead of setting grace and nature against each other, Kuyper distinguished between creation and re-creation. "Nature" is understood as everything that is rooted in and functions according to the original creation. In spite of the fall and subsequent curse under which creation suffers, common grace averts the deadly consequences of the curse and renders possible and certain "the continued, be it afflicted,

20. Ibid., 172.
21. Ibid., 173.

existence of all that came from the original creation."[22] Re-creation, on the other hand, belongs to the domain of special grace and not only restrains things but also creates them. Kuyper further clarified the distinction:

> It is altogether a *new Creation* which, though linked with the original (for it is *Re-creation*), in its newness cannot be explained from the old. The inaccurate antithesis between *nature* and *grace* that has come down to us from medieval theology can be used only if qualified by the addition that nature, cursed as it is by itself, can endure only by the action of common grace. The Reformed principle produces a much purer distinction between the things that originate from the Creation and the things that originate from Re-creation. That far-reaching distinction is this: in common grace there is never anything new, never anything but what can be explained from the original creation; on the other hand, in special grace nothing arises from creation but everything is *new* and can only be explained from the new Creation or Re-creation.[23]

Kuyper revised or, better, replaced the distinction between nature and grace with his Reformed principle. The previous paragraph shows how Kuyper brought nature and grace together by reference to Christ in order to reveal creation as graced. Then in this reference, Kuyper offered the Reformed distinction as a way to compartmentalize grace as common and special. With that principle, creation (nature) is perceived as fallen and unable to produce anything new, but this does not preclude development. Rather, while there is an inability to create (or make new) in a supernatural sense (as in re-creation), the possibility of cultivation remains as a result of common grace.

It is in relation to the potential for creation's development that Kuyper articulated the relationship between common grace and history. As a result of the constancy of common grace, history is possible. In making reference to history, Kuyper encouraged the development of creation. In fact, he spoke of it as inevitable and beneficial:

> Common grace opens a history, unlocks an enormous space of time, triggers a vast and long-lasting stream of events, in a word, precipitates a series of successive centuries. If that series of centuries is not directed toward an endless, unvarying repetition of the same things, then over the course of those centuries there has to be constant change,

22. Ibid., 174.
23. Ibid.

modification, transformation in human life. Though it pass through periods of deepening darkness, this change has to ignite ever more light, consistently enrich human life, and so bear the character of perpetual development from less to more, a progressively fuller unfolding of life. If one pictures the distance that exists even now between the life of a Hottentot in his kraal and the life of a highly refined family in European society, one can measure that process in the blink of an eye. And though people imagine at the end of every century that its progress has been so astonishing that further progress can hardly be imagined, every century nevertheless teaches us that the new things added each time surpass all that has been imagined before. How has the nineteenth century not changed and enriched our human life and blessed it with new conveniences![24]

Common grace makes progress possible. There is a constant, preservative aspect of common grace that leads to a progressive aspect. Such a view of progress was apparently rare among Christians, for Kuyper criticized Christian resistance to social-architectural development in society. He urged his readers to recognize "that Christians, by refusing to participate in that development, were the reason why morally and religiously that development often took a wrong turn."[25] Kuyper listed "a variety of Anabaptist and Methodist influences"[26] as the culprits for this state of affairs. Rather than opposing progress and engagement in society and culture, Christians should play a central role in directing the development of life, helping to construct a society that operates in accordance with the divine ordinances of creation.

Kuyper also argued that the development of humanity is part of the divine plan. History, the development of life, has a significance and a purpose because God works in and on the horizon of centuries past, present, and future. If God is not at work in history, then, Kuyper

24. Ibid., 174–75. This quote reveals Kuyper as a man of his time, particularly in his enthusiastic view of progress.

25. Ibid., 175.

26. Kuyper did not mean Methodism denominationally as much as religious influences that called Christians away from life in the world. Kuyper tended to resist the influences of pietism, yet he wrote many devotional works that aimed to cultivate the inner, spiritual life. In this regard, Richard Mouw's chapter "Lessons from the 'Labadists'" is significant. Mouw addresses the Reformed tendency to use the term *Anabaptist* as a cruel name for one's opponents, though in fact there is much more in common between Reformed and Anabaptists than acknowledged. See Richard Mouw, *He Shines in All That's Fair: Culture and Common Grace* (Grand Rapids: Eerdmans, 2001), 20–29.

suggested, one has to credit the development of society to the work of Satan or humans.[27] To support this perspective, he argued that it is biblical. "Scripture speaks of 'the consummation of the ages' [Matt. 13:39–40], a term that does not mean the centuries will terminate at some point but that they are directed toward a final goal and that everything contained in those centuries is linked to that final goal."[28] The divinely ordained *telos* of creation history reveals the import and larger purpose of ongoing development.

The process of such development is not effortless or painless. Though the process contains considerable suffering and misery, the experience of distress is the means by which God prods people toward advancement. While it can appear that the relationship between distress and development means that suffering and misery are themselves means of common grace, such is not the case. Rather, Kuyper perceived such difficulties through the divine decree and hence viewed them positively as a part of God's ultimate purpose, though not as gracious means. In regard to such difficulties, Kuyper articulated a view of creation's potential by accenting a form of progressive general revelation:

> We must rather recognize that suffering is *the enemy* against which God calls us to do battle. However—and here the shoe pinches—God does not reveal all at once what he alone can show us: the means by which we may protect ourselves from and resist that suffering. Successively, in the course of centuries, God has over and over inspired us to discover something new, giving us a clearer glimpse of those means. In this respect Noah was farther along than Adam, Moses than Noah, Solomon than Moses, and continuing in that line, we are farther along than our ancestors. It is not as if something totally new were created. All that God has disclosed to us already lay stored up in the creation from the beginning. But we did not know it and did not see it, and God has used the centuries, step by step, to help us discover ever more, ever new things by which our human life could be enriched. . . . *That* has been the development of our race; therein alone lay the real component of progress.[29]

Creation is like a plant that has developed from a seed and continues to bloom and yield better benefits for humanity. For the human race

27. Kuyper, "Common Grace," 175.
28. Ibid.
29. Ibid., 175–76.

at large, life improves as a result of tilling the soil of creation, made fertile through common grace.

Kuyper urged that as this process of development goes on toward the ultimate consummation, the stewardship of creation must be taken seriously. "Not a year, not a day, not an hour can be spared. For all those centuries God has restlessly continued his work in our human race, in the totality of the life of this world. Nothing in it is purposeless or redundant."[30] It is important to attend to life outside the church walls, even if one cannot directly demonstrate its significance for the faith. Regardless, Kuyper argued that it has meaning because it is part of God's plan to "actualize everything he had put into this world at the time of creation, to insist on its realization, to develop it so completely that the full sum of its vital energies may enter the light of day at the consummation of the world."[31]

If common grace is God's work in the world so that the potential of creation is realized, how does this occur? It occurs through social-architectural construction, through cultural development. In spelling this out, Kuyper again reflected on the *telos* of creation and stated that the development of creation, the terrain of common grace, has a distinct and separate goal from that of salvation.[32] The core of this goal is tied to an understanding of the *imago Dei* that is corporate in nature. Rather than limiting creation in the image of God to individuals, Kuyper argued that the entire human race is corporately the bearer of the divine image. With this approach, he argued that the image of God can be mirrored more fully. A key aspect of this mirroring is the development of social life. In support of his perspective, Kuyper stated:

> The social side of man's creation in God's image has nothing to do with salvation nor in any way with each person's state before God. This social element tells us only that in creating human beings in his likeness God deposited an infinite number of nuclei for high human development in our nature and that these nuclei cannot develop except *through the social bond between people*. From this viewpoint the highly ramified development of humanity acquires a significance of its own, an independent goal, a reason for being aside from the issue of salvation. If it has pleased God to mirror the richness of his image

30. Ibid., 176.
31. Ibid., 175.
32. Ibid., 178.

in the social multiplicity and fullness of our race, and if he himself has deposited the nuclei of that development in human nature, *then* the brilliance of his image *has to* appear. Then that richness *may not* remain concealed, those nuclei *may not* dry up and wither, and humanity will *have* to remain on earth for as long as it takes to unfold as fully and richly as necessary those nuclei of human potential.[33]

Human development is a necessity that must reach its goal because it is a part of God's plan to see the full glory of the divine image reflected in creation.

Human development is made possible by common grace. The process of reflecting the divine image with increasingly greater accuracy is part of developing the entire creation. The project can be understood as a social-architectural task that aims to improve the conditions of life. Again, Kuyper understood this task as separate from the task of salvation, though he argued that God is directly involved through common grace:

The supreme Artisan and Architect will want all that has gone into his design to be realized and stand before him in a splendid edifice. God will take delight in that high human development. He himself will bring it about and into view. Then he will seek in it his own glorification. The control and harnessing of nature by civilization, enlightenment, and progress, by science and art, by a variety of enterprises and industry will be entirely separate from the totally other development in holiness and integrity; indeed, that *exterior* development may even clash openly with an *interior* development in holiness and become a temptation to the believer. Still, that exterior development in holiness has to continue and be completed to bring the *work of God* in our race to full visible realization.[34]

33. Ibid.
34. Ibid., 178–79. A couple of things are important to note here. First, one can ask whether Kuyper's statement about the temptation of exterior development gives considerable pause to those who find public engagement a questionable enterprise. If it is a temptation, is it not possible that it could lead many well-intentioned Christians to a faith so focused on public concerns that the gospel of special grace is ignored? Clearly, Kuyper's view is that public engagement is a task that must be performed, though with sobriety and a view of God's glory as primary. Second, for Kuyper, the teleology of creation requires positive development, but it is also necessary for evil to flourish in its development so that the Antichrist can appear and then the consummation of the ages. "At the moment of its destruction Babylon—that is, the world power which evolved from human life—will exhibit not the image of a barbarous horde nor the image of coarse bestiality but, on the contrary, a picture of the highest develop-

From Kuyper's perspective, it is mandatory that the purpose of common grace reach fulfillment. In fact, he credited common grace with making the primary creation ordinance an attainable goal. Though there is the circumstance of a fallen created order, common grace enables humans to achieve dominion over nature. Indeed, without common grace, human development over history does not make much sense.[35]

If common grace encourages the social-architectural task, how should Christians approach this task? As expressed in the previous chapter, Kuyper aimed for a form of social engagement that respects sphere sovereignty. Yet he also believed that the church should influence society. In urging the church to have an influence, Kuyper, consistent with sphere sovereignty, argued against a national church. From the standpoint of grace, Kuyper articulated the alternatives:

> Now if only *grace* can avert a curse and block the superior power of the demonic, then one of two things must happen: either grace must be at work outside the church, or all that lies outside and cannot be absorbed in the church remains bereft of grace and so helplessly in bondage to the curse. "Exorcism" is then the natural means applied by the church to break this power, to withdraw a part of the world from bondage to the curse and bring it under grace. Even the plot of land ground at stake must then be consecrated, for there too the world is divided in two parts: one *consecrated,* the other *not;* and all that is not consecrated remains outside the sphere of grace. All this ends, however, the moment one sees that there definitely *is* a *grace* operating outside the church, that there is *grace* even where it does not lead to eternal salvation, and that we are therefore duty-bound to honor an operation of divine grace in human civic life by which the curse of sin, and sin itself, is restrained even though the link with salvation is lacking.[36]

Common grace provides a way, an obligation, to pursue the social-architectural task. The church spreads its influence by in-

---

ment of which human life is capable. It will display the most refined forms, the most magnificent unfolding of wealth and splendor, the fullest brilliance of all that makes life dazzling and glorious. From this we know that 'common grace' will continue to function to the end. Only when common grace has spurred the full emergence of all the powers inherent in human life will 'the man of sin' find the level terrain needed to expand this power. Only then will the end be near and judgment come over him suddenly, on a single day, in the span of a single hour" (ibid., 181).

35. Ibid., 179.
36. Ibid., 192.

direct means, not by the imposition of a particular confession.[37]
The development of society occurs by having Christians present in
every area of life who promote religious liberty, oppose the introduction or propagation of pagan concepts and ideas into the legal
and sociopolitical fabric of the country, and expand the dominance
of more noble and pure ideas in society.[38] This task can meet with
success when the recipients of special grace cultivate the terrain of
common grace.

Kuyper contended that as a result of common grace it is possible
to have a "Christian" nation. By using such language, Kuyper did
not have in mind a theocracy or even a nation whose population is
primarily regenerate. Rather, such a nation has existed when "special
grace in the church and among believers exerted so strong a formative
influence on common grace that common grace thereby attained its
highest development."[39] In such a nation, the social architecture of
the country exhibits the influence of the Christian faith. As a result,
such nations have improved the status of women, abolished slavery,
maintained public virtue, and demonstrated compassion for the
poor.[40] For Kuyper, the best society will result from a responsible
and faithful stewardship of common grace.

In addition to providing the seedbed for sociopolitical engagement and development, common grace provides the gifts and talents
distributed to all human beings irrespective of their faith. Common
grace not only makes artistic abilities available to all, as stated in the
previous chapter, but also provides gifts such as the intellect. Concerning the latter, Kuyper remarked in the Stone Lectures that

> precious treasures have come down to us from the old heathen civi-
> lization. In Plato you find pages which you devour. Cicero fascinates
> you and bears you along by his noble tone and stirs up in you holy
> sentiments. And if you consider your own surroundings, that which
> is reported to you, and that which you derive from the studies and
> literary productions of professed infidels, how much there is which
> attracts you, with which you sympathize and which you admire. It is
> not exclusively the spark of genius or the splendor of talent, which
> excites your pleasure in the words and actions of unbelievers, but it

37. Ibid., 197.
38. Ibid.
39. Ibid., 199.
40. Ibid.

is often their beauty of character, their zeal, their devotion, their love, their candor, their faithfulness and their sense of honesty.[41]

Common grace is the reason there is so much to admire from non-Christians. Though total depravity exists in the sense that all aspects of human life bear the effects of the fall, the restraint of sin has kept the human race from the unbridled effects of sin. In a sense, common grace has domesticated humanity. In this state of domestication, the abilities given to humanity have been developed and have flourished over the course of history, resulting in such things as orderly societies and a minimum of horrible, sinful atrocities.[42] Of great significance for Kuyper is that the appreciation of non-Christian art and intellectual achievements is an appreciation of the created order. This must be qualified, however, with the reminder that Kuyper's doctrine of the antithesis kept him from uncritical appreciation of non-Christian thought and activity. Kuyper was concerned with making creation, the terrain of common grace, a place worthy of Christian engagement, but not in a careless fashion.

Kuyper sought to motivate his constituency to public engagement, as demonstrated in the previous chapter. The doctrine of common grace is the theological foundation and motivation for public engagement. Common grace restrains sin, enables historical development and progress, and makes a positive view of creation possible. Common grace enables and encourages the social-architectural task. As S. U. Zuidema has said:

> Common grace supplies the believer with the material for fulfilling his calling to be culturally formative and to fight the battle of the Lord in the world of culture. The sphere of common grace . . . is the area where Christian scholarship, Christian politics, Christian social action and individual Christian activity are to be developed. Common grace provides the platform, as it were, on which these cultural tasks are to be acted out. Common grace is *the presupposition of the possibility of* Christian cultural activity.[43]

41. Kuyper, *Calvinism*, 159–60.
42. Ibid., 163–64. It is worth noting again that Kuyper's view of progress, prior to a century with two world wars, is highly optimistic, leading him to conclude that humans would rarely perpetrate grand atrocities.
43. Zuidema, "Common Grace and Christian Action in Abraham Kuyper," 57.

Points of Concern

Though Kuyper formulated his doctrine of common grace with the intention of motivating the Christian (particularly Reformed) populace to action in the public realm, this doctrine has raised some points of concern. Five figures in particular have raised issues pertinent to the scope of this book.[44]

In his *Calvinistic Concept of Culture*, Henry Van Til argues that Kuyper's doctrine of common grace as the foundation of culture and history is too speculative and lacks scriptural support. In particular, Van Til criticizes Kuyper's position that common grace came about so that creation would not fall into chaos. In his view, the cultural action of believers is not a common grace operation but merely the restoration of humanity's dominion mandate made possible through Christ: "To say that the world continues its existence due to the common grace of God is to put the cart before the horse, since God gave his promises to our first parents and also to Noah on the basis of his purpose to redeem the world in and through Jesus Christ."[45] According to Van Til's perspective, the divine decrees include the fall and God's plan to enable the fulfillment of the cultural mandate through redemption. Believing there is a separate purpose for common grace, as distinct from special grace, is unfounded speculation.

Another criticism comes from Jacob Klapwijk, who argues that Kuyper's contrast between common and special grace lends itself to "a spiritualizing dualism, a kind of mysticism that expresses itself in a bifurcated orientation to the hereafter and the present."[46] It is not always clear that God's action in common grace is ultimately for the sake of Christ. In Kuyper's writings, at times the purposes of common and special grace converge and at other times they remain separate. As noted in the previous chapter, this tension can be observed in the Stone Lectures, and Kuyper does not resolve the dilemma. Klapwijk, in fairness to Kuyper, also acknowledges that this tension reflects the tension of Kuyper's personal life:

44. Though Cornelius Van Til wrote on common grace, his focus was mostly soteriological (such as points of contact between Christians and non-Christians and reconciling the universal offer of salvation with election). Therefore, his work is not included here. See Van Til, *Common Grace and the Gospel*.

45. Van Til, *Calvinistic Concept of Culture*, 231.

46. Klapwijk, "Antithesis and Common Grace," 173.

In part, his work echoes the mystery of the born-again heart, the sigh of the weary pilgrim who yearns for his eternal home. In part, he is driven to work with extraordinary vigor at the unfolding of God's creation in state, society, and science. And even here his ideas seem sometimes at odds with each other. At times he regards the creation mandate as a common human task in which Christians and non-Christians struggle side by side. At such times it seems as if the terrain of common grace is equivalent to the realm of nature in medieval Scholasticism. At other times Kuyper is sure that the great cultural mandate leaves no room for cooperation with the non-Christian; he is sure that this mandate proclaims the Lordship of Jesus Christ over the whole world and that it must therefore be translated into a program of organized Christian action in all areas of life, including science and philosophy.[47]

Klapwijk's observation reveals that Kuyper was not always consistent. Yet it is important to remember that Kuyper was not primarily concerned with writing an academic treatment of common grace. In spite of his references to core principles, he was not always concerned with presenting a balance between his theological emphases in every article or speech. His concerns were simultaneously theological and practical because his objective was to motivate his constituency to action. Depending on the occasion, Kuyper's goals called for emphasizing a general appreciation of creation or for rallying the troops to articulate and implement a uniquely Christian approach in the public arena. When reading Kuyper, it is helpful to remember that his works reflect their occasional nature, and the emphases of both common grace and antithesis were needed in his historical situation.[48]

Cornelis van der Kooi raises concerns related to sociocultural development and Christology in his appraisal of Kuyper's doctrine of common grace. While acknowledging that Kuyper's doctrine affirms human cultural activity, van der Kooi reflects an ambivalence toward development. "Two world wars, various outbursts of genocide, threats to our natural environment by unrestrained economic growth have tempered the optimism and kindled distrust of the faith in progress that was so characteristic of Kuyper's worldview."[49] Though one may affirm the place of culture and the centrality of divine action in the life-affirming aspects of development, an attitude of caution is

47. Ibid., 173–74.
48. See Heslam, *Creating a Christian Worldview,* 117–23.
49. Cornelis van der Kooi, "A Theology of Culture: A Critical Appraisal of Kuyper's Doctrine of Common Grace," in *Kuyper Reconsidered,* 100.

required. Rather than adhering to Kuyper's view that the presence of potential in creation necessitates or requires fulfillment, van der Kooi suggests that we accept the positive aspects of development as gifts of God while also considering the vulnerability of humans and the world. In this regard, it is important to recognize that some technological developments, for example, can be undesirable because they may reach the peak of their destructive power. With this perspective, it is possible to view life in the world as meaningful while not doing so with unbridled optimism.

In regard to Christology, van der Kooi expresses concern over Kuyper's distinction between the eternal Son and the incarnate Son. The distinction, he argues, threatens the unity of God by leading to a consideration of culture and historical progress apart from the being and work of Jesus. In contrast, van der Kooi argues:

> I would want to defend the proposition that God is certainly more than the Son, and His works are not wholly comprehended in the work of salvation, but also that nothing more can be said about God in all his works outside of his acts in Jesus Christ. Since the life of Jesus, his crucifixion and resurrection, it is impossible to think of God outside of this history. When the New Testament speaks of Christ as the agent of creation, that is not thought of apart from his work on earth, but his power (*exousia*) as the agent of creation characterizes his life on earth, his crucifixion and resurrection.[50]

This approach unites the eternal Son and the incarnate Son and demonstrates why culture and history are rooted in the incarnation as well as the eternal decree before time. This critique contains echoes of Klapwijk's concern regarding Kuyper's tensions between common and special grace but with a greater christological focus.

Is it possible to address these concerns, all of which focus primarily on a separation of the work of Christ in redemption from a general grace of creation? One answer is found in S. U. Zuidema's article "Common Grace and Christian Action in Abraham Kuyper." Zuidema argues that the path to resolving Kuyper's tensions lies in stressing Kuyper's doctrine of particular grace in relation to common grace. While acknowledging that Kuyper argued for distinct goals for the two forms of grace, Zuidema insists that "if there is to be a restoration of Kuyper's doctrine of common grace in which

50. Ibid.

the contradictions no longer occur, it should be undertaken in no other way than in the way of a full-fledged elaboration of the things Kuyper wrote concerning Christ and concerning particular grace that 'restores creation in its root.'"[51] Zuidema's strategy is clear. By placing greater weight on the restorative power of particular grace, common grace no longer has a separate purpose but rather serves the ends of particular grace. In this view, common grace is the terrain for Christian action, even for Christian warfare:

> Common grace should then be confessed as a work of God whereby He upholds his creation, maintains His creation ordinances, and thus opens the way for the militant as well as suffering church to fight her warfare *pro Rege,* throughout this age, with the weapons God in His common grace has provided her—weapons that are forged, in spite of the impulse that is not of God, also by unbelievers, who no less than believers are fitted by God's common grace with gifts and talents for their tasks, tasks which they perform, whatever they intend and whatsoever they will, in the service of particular grace.[52]

From Zuidema's perspective, Kuyper's doctrine of common grace is useful for the very purpose Kuyper intended: to encourage a positive view of creation and to affirm engagement in the public realm. Though he may not have resolved his tensions to the satisfaction of all supporters and critics, Kuyper did provide a theological rationale for public engagement that can be salvaged without substantial alterations.

Given the fact that Kuyper was a supralapsarian,[53] Zuidema's response makes perfect sense. Since the glory of God in carrying out the decree of election is central to the supralapsarian position, those who detected in Kuyper the tendency to separate the purposes of common grace and particular grace would have found him to be inconsistent. From an infralapsarian perspective, however, Richard

51. Zuidema, "Common Grace and Christian Action in Abraham Kuyper," 100.
52. Ibid., 101.
53. The supralapsarian position in Reformed theology argues that God, prior to creation, first decreed the election to salvation and reprobation and then subsequently decreed the creation, fall, and salvation through Christ. Infralapsarians, the majority position in Reformed theology, argue that God decreed creation first, then the fall, and then only subsequently the decrees for election, reprobation, and salvation in Christ. A summary can be found in Mouw, *He Shines in All That's Fair,* 54–55.

Mouw expresses another way to respond to the concerns regarding Kuyper's doctrine of common grace.

According to Mouw, the infralapsarian view takes a more complex approach in the way it treats God's self-glorifying designs. Since the first decree is to create the world, followed by the decrees of election, reprobation, and salvation through Christ, infralapsarians emphasize the "manyness" of the decree. Rather than making one decree central and hence the ultimate purpose for all that follows, the infralapsarian position allows for a multiplicity in divine purposes. "There is no reason why, for example, an infralapsarian could not view God as taking delight in a display of athletic prowess because of ultimate purposes that stand alongside of, rather than being subservient to, the goal of bringing about election and reprobation."[54] If there is such multiplicity in the divine purposes, then the infralapsarian position provides a way to understand common grace as having a God-glorifying purpose without necessarily linking it to the particular grace of redemption. While it is true that Kuyper was a committed supralapsarian, one way to get beyond some of the conflict in Kuyper's approach is to consider it from the infralapsarian perspective.

It is interesting to note that the majority of concerns raised here are in some way christological. In reflecting on the divine decree, the tensions between common and special grace, and the unity of God, the focus is on the Second Person of the Trinity. Christology is obviously central, yet the Second Person of the Trinity is not the only active member in common grace. The Holy Spirit, the Third Person of the Trinity, is in fact also central to common grace and thus to Kuyper's public theology, as will now be shown.

The Work of the Holy Spirit in Creation: The Missing Link

Kuyper referred to Christ as the root of common grace, as mentioned above. Yet it is also possible to demonstrate that the work of the Holy Spirit in creation was equally essential to his theological rationale for public engagement. The language Kuyper used to describe the Spirit's activity in the biophysical order overlapped with his description of the operation of common grace.

54. Ibid., 61–62.

Kuyper wrote *The Work of the Holy Spirit* as a series for *De Heraut*. It was later published in book form in 1888 and translated into English in 1900. It predated Kuyper's initial work on common grace by seven years. It is interesting to observe that though Kuyper's work on the Spirit clearly reflects the language of common grace, the direct connection is not made in his discussion of common grace. Though a matter of speculation, this could have been the result of his concern to focus on the relationship between Christ and common grace, though his efforts in that regard did not free him from criticism, as seen above.

How did Kuyper articulate his doctrine of the Holy Spirit in creation? For Kuyper, there were three aspects of the Spirit's activity in creation. First, the Spirit performs a perfecting function in the creative act. Citing 1 Corinthians 8:6 and Romans 11:36, Kuyper made a distinction among the members of the Trinity, stating that the Father is the power of initial generation or creation, the Son is the power of arrangement or organization, and the Spirit is the power of perfection. In terms of the biophysical order, the Father spoke and produced the material of creation, the Son formed and ordered creation, and the Spirit's role is to bring the potentialities of creation to their most complete end. Kuyper stated, "The creature is made not simply to exist or to adorn some niche in the universe like a statue. Rather was everything created with a purpose and a destiny; our creation will be complete only when we have become what God designed. . . . Thus to lead the creature to its destiny, to cause it to develop according to its nature, to make it perfect, is the proper work of the Holy Spirit."[55] What was the end of this perfection for Kuyper? The glory of God.[56] A central purpose of the Spirit's cosmic work is to be immanent in creation and to promote the progress and development of the created order toward its proper *telos*.

55. Abraham Kuyper, *The Work of the Holy Spirit,* trans. Henri De Vries (Grand Rapids: Eerdmans, 1941), 21. On pp. 29–30, Kuyper restates the idea by addressing Genesis 1:2: "Hence the material forces of the universe do not proceed from the Holy Spirit, nor did He deposit in matter the dormant seeds and germs of life. His special task begins only *after* the creation of matter with the germs of life in it. The Hebrew text shows that the work of the Holy Spirit moving upon the face of the waters was similar to that of the parent bird which with outspread wings hovers over its young to cherish and cover them. The figure implies that not only the earth existed but the germs of life within it; and that the Holy Spirit impregnating these germs caused the life to come forth in order to lead it to its destiny."

56. Ibid., 22–24.

Second, Kuyper viewed the Spirit as the animating principle of all life. Using Psalm 104:30 as a reference, Kuyper pointed to the fact that the Spirit not only regenerates the elect but also gives life to the biophysical order. This work is invisible and not often associated with the Spirit, an oversight Kuyper intended to correct.

> How intangible are the forces of nature, how full of majesty the forces of magnetism! But life underlies all. Even through the apparently dead trunk sighs an imperceptible breath. From the unfathomable depths of all an inward, hidden principle works upward and outward. It shows in nature, much more in man and angel. And what is this quickening and animating principle but the Holy Spirit? . . . This inward, invisible something is God's direct touch. There is in us and in every creature a point where the living God touches us to uphold us; for nothing exists without being *upheld* by Almighty God from moment to moment. In the elect this point is their spiritual life; in the rational creature his rational consciousness; and in all creatures, whether rational or not, their life principle. And as the Holy Spirit is the Person in the Holy Trinity whose office it is to effect this direct touch and fellowship with the creature in his inmost being, it is He who *dwells* in the hearts of the elect; who *animates* every rational being; who sustains the *principle of life* in every creature.[57]

No life can be sustained apart from the Spirit's involvement, apart from divine vitalization. Further, even the rational faculties of all humans owe their normal function to the Spirit's animating work.

The third aspect of the Spirit's role in creation is the restraint of sin. The Spirit constantly antagonizes sin and keeps creation from falling into chaos. This is a vital function as the Spirit moves creation to its end of glorifying God.[58]

Kuyper's view of the cosmic activities of the Spirit is implicitly linked to common grace. In describing the role of common grace in creation, Kuyper made comments that overlapped with his statements concerning the Spirit's role in creation. It is relevant at this point to repeat Kuyper's definition of the doctrine in the Stone Lectures, where he says that there is a "*common grace* by which God, maintaining the life of the world, relaxes the curse which rests upon it, arrests its process of corruption, and thus allows the untramelled development of our life in which to glorify Himself as Creator."[59] As described

57. Ibid., 25–26.
58. Ibid., 24.
59. Kuyper, *Calvinism*, 30–31.

above, Kuyper understood the cosmic work of the Spirit as that which seeks God's glory in a perfected *telos,* upholds and maintains the world, and resists the sinful curse on creation so that creation may develop and move toward its intended end. This aligns with the purpose of common grace, revealing the Spirit's role as the energizing force of these capacities. Referring to Acts 17:25, 28, Kuyper stated, "There is no sun, moon, nor star, no material, plant, or animal, and in much higher sense, no man, skill, gift, or talent unless God touch and support them all. It is this act of coming into immediate contact with every creature, animate or inanimate, organic or inorganic, rational or irrational, that, according to the profound conception of the Word of God, is performed not by the Father, nor by the Son, but by the Holy Spirit."[60] This language reveals that the Spirit is the dynamic force of common grace.

In addition, as mentioned above, Kuyper attributed art and other gifts and talents to common grace. This is the subject of the eighth chapter in *The Work of the Holy Spirit,* where Kuyper wrote of the Holy Spirit as their source. The ability to govern, the capacity to realize the potential of material creation in art, and the ability to excel in some office or profession are vital capacities for public theology that result from a general gifting of the Spirit. As Kuyper stated:

> The Spirit's working shows not only in ordinary skilled labor, but also in the higher spheres of human knowledge and mental activity. . . . This talent, this individual genius so intimately connected with man's personality, is a *gift.* No power in the world can create it in the man that possesses it not. The child is born with or without it; if without it, no education nor severity—not even ambition—can call it forth. But as the gift of grace is freely bestowed by the sovereign God, so is also the gift of genius. When people pray, let them not forget to ask the Lord to raise up among them men of talent, heroes of art and of office.[61]

The relationship between the Spirit and common grace is clear in this instance.

As stated previously, Kuyper also understood common grace as that which compels people to attend to and develop creation responsibly. "And for our relation *to the world:* the recognition that

60. Kuyper, *Work of the Holy Spirit,* 44.
61. Ibid., 41.

in the whole world the curse is restrained by grace, that the life of the world is to be honored in its independence, and that we must, in every domain, discover the treasures and develop the potencies hidden by God in nature and in human life."[62] This language corresponds with Kuyper's understanding of the teleology of the Spirit's work in creation. It reveals that the Spirit's work in prompting the development of life can also be understood as a catalyst for history.

As stated above, the Spirit's cosmic activity is the dynamic element of common grace. Based on the statements above, it is clear that the Spirit can be understood as the agent of or the one who provides the context for common grace. Kuyper's description of common grace speaks of the restraint of sin, the animation and sustenance of the biophysical order, and the development of creation to its goal, the same kind of language used to describe the Spirit's cosmic work. While Kuyper indeed spoke of Christ as the root of common grace, the Spirit was equally vital. Though Christ as *Logos* is the source of common grace, the Spirit's life-giving, life-sustaining touch is the dynamic element of common grace. As such, the Spirit's work in creation can be understood as a central yet unacknowledged force underlying Kuyper's public theology. This leads to the conclusion that the Spirit as the agent of common grace is the driving force behind total engagement with the world and that the Spirit's cosmic work in common grace calls for responsible stewardship of the created order. Common grace calls for fervent involvement in creation but with a fervor tempered by a great respect for creation.

The Holy Spirit's work in creation can be understood as a "missing link" in many understandings of Kuyper's public theology and in those Calvinistic views that accent the sovereignty of God and redemption in Christ, with the Holy Spirit used only to interpret Scripture and apply the benefits of redemption. While there has been much discussion of the relationship between special grace and common grace in Kuyper's theology, there has been minimal if any discussion of his view of the Spirit's cosmic work in relation to common grace. Though the connection has been made clear here, a further task remains. Kuyper was concerned to recontextualize doctrine for his era, and the usefulness of his insights for the present age requires that such work continue. The next chapter focuses on advancing the discussion of the Spirit's work in creation and the approach to public theology that results.

62. Kuyper, *Calvinism,* 33.

4

THE SPIRIT AND CREATION
STEWARDSHIP

ADVANCING THE DOCTRINE OF THE SPIRIT
IN CREATION

Abraham Kuyper had no desire merely to repristinate Calvinism. He sought to articulate and further develop the tradition of Reformed Christianity in a manner that addressed his context. It is in the same spirit that this chapter seeks to advance reflection on the doctrine of the Holy Spirit in regard to creation and public theology. At the beginning, it is necessary to repeat a concern about pneumatology raised in the first chapter. The work of John McIntyre called for a pneumatological perspective or logic articulated in a distinctive fashion. An emphasis on distinction does not mean that the search is for a monistic pneumatology but rather for a fully trinitarian perspective on the Spirit. This can occur by distinguishing the work of the Holy Spirit from Christology in a manner that illuminates the unique role of the Spirit, specifically in regard to creation in this instance. How can one take such steps forward? McIntyre's work offers the following suggestion for understanding the Spirit's work in relation to common grace and non-Christians:

If we speak of their being sustained even in their rebellion, but in all their daily living, through "common grace," it is perhaps preferable to construe their position in terms of existence within the domain of the gracious Holy Spirit, where they live and act within the structures, the laws, the principles, the sanctions, the mercy, forgiveness and comfort, which are the expression of his sovereignty.[1]

Language regarding existence within the domain of the gracious Spirit provides a way to construe not only the lives of humans but the entire biophysical order as sustained by the Spirit, though McIntyre does not go beyond this reflection to speak of implications for sociocultural development. The work of Dutch theologian Arnold A. Van Ruler provides a fruitful dialogue that can advance theological reflection on the Spirit's work in creation. Before proceeding, however, it is important to recognize that Van Ruler was a critic of Abraham Kuyper. As a result, it may seem questionable to use his work. This is not the problem that it appears to be, however, because Van Ruler's pneumatology is not in conflict with the aim of recontextualizing Kuyper's doctrine of the Spirit in creation.

Van Ruler and "Pneumatological Categories"

The second and third chapters in *Calvinist Trinitarianism and Theocentric Politics,* a collection of essays by Van Ruler, are particularly relevant to the task of developing reflection on pneumatology. At the outset, it is important to note that Van Ruler's focus is primarily soteriological. The constructive task here, therefore, is to find aspects of his theological reflection that can be transposed to the domain of the Spirit's work in creation and common grace. Chapter 2, titled "Structural Differences between the Christological and Pneumatological Perspectives," attempts to arrive at a fully pneumatological understanding of salvation and will serve as the primary source for the task of recontextualization. For Van Ruler, this attempt is important because salvation is made effective for humans in the mode of the Holy Spirit.[2] In making his point, Van Ruler describes several structural differences that he observes between the perspectives of

1. John McIntyre, *The Shape of Pneumatology: Studies in the Doctrine of the Holy Spirit* (Edinburgh: T & T Clark, 1997), 284.
2. Arnold A. Van Ruler, *Calvinist Trinitarianism and Theocentric Politics: Essays toward a Public Theology,* trans. John Bolt (Lewiston, N.Y.: Edwin Mellen, 1989), 28.

pneumatology and Christology. By speaking of "structural differences," Van Ruler means the following:

> One cannot gratuitously derive the structure of pneumatological dogma from christological dogma. This was done rather easily in the fourth century in terms of immanent-trinitarian relations, and thereafter usually in terms of the salvation-historical relations. Nevertheless, the reality of "God in us" is too different a reality from "God in Christ" to permit this, just as within the immanent trinity the Spirit is in no sense parallel, for example, as a brother or sister, to the Son. Pneumatological dogma has its own distinct structure in comparison with christological dogma. . . . Whenever one considers Christian salvation, and the relationship between God and humanity described in that salvation, from a pneumatological perspective, one must deal with different laws and apply different rules than when one considers it from a christological perspective.[3]

If it is possible to observe such structural differences soteriologically, it should be possible to articulate structural distinctives in the Spirit's work in creation. This is not achieved by asserting a direct parallelism between the Spirit's work in humanity and in creation but by noting that the insight concerning structural differences in regard to soteriology can also apply to creation and common grace. This opens an avenue to a more fully trinitarian understanding of God's work in creation by more fully distinguishing the Spirit's work.

As noted, Van Ruler's focus is salvation. As a result, some of the structural differences are not applicable to the Spirit's work in creation and common grace, so they will not be included here. The first structural difference that has implications for this chapter can be gleaned from the distinction that Van Ruler makes between the christological category of assumption versus the pneumatological category of adoption. In the incarnation, Christ assumed human nature, while in the work of salvation, the Spirit does not assume the nature of humans but rather adopts them. "In assumption, the human nature is added to; in adoption, human beings are placed in relationship over against God."[4] The implication Van Ruler draws from this that has relevance for the Spirit's work in creation is that the Spirit seeks to take form in humans, in terms of their thought,

3. Ibid., 28–29.
4. Ibid., 33.

volition, and activity. If this is transposed to the realm of creation and common grace, it leads to a way to articulate the relationship that the Spirit has to history and sociocultural development. In the same way that the Spirit acts to form certain characteristics in regenerate humans, could it be that the Spirit's activity in common grace, particularly in its teleological aspect, leads to the formation of certain forms of society?[5] Kuyper argued that common grace not only made history possible but also leads to a society in which life is increasingly manageable. As the Spirit moves creation to its *telos,* it may be that common grace enables the possibility of better social architecture for human life. Through the Spirit-enabled discovery and development of creation ordinances, it may be possible to arrive at cultural, legal, political, and environmental values and policies that yield forms of society that provide a glimpse of the New Jerusalem.

This does not mean that the category of adoption is itself suitable for our purposes. It may be better to understand this teleological aspect as a facet of *creatio continua,* because the Spirit's work in common grace serves as the means for the formation of societies that reflect creation ordinances. This leads to the inquiries, Does *creatio continua* lead to not only the discovery of but also the construction of ordinances that yield such societies? Is the work of the Spirit in common grace so dynamic in character that creation is considered to have not only latent potential but also numerous sociocultural

5. The teleological aspect of the Spirit is also seen in the work of Colin Gunton (see chap. 1 above). A distinct difference between Kuyper and Gunton is that Gunton suggests that the Spirit leads creation to return ultimately to God, while Kuyper speaks in the language of re-creation. For Kuyper, the Spirit is leading creation to its goal of being all that God intended from the beginning, but that goal is not understood eschatologically as a return to God. Instead, the transformed creation will exist as a part of the new heavens and new earth. See Abraham Kuyper, *The Work of the Holy Spirit,* trans. Hendrik de Vries (Grand Rapids: Eerdmans, 1941), 8–11, 19–21. In his third chapter, Van Ruler also questions the idea of the Spirit leading the creation back to God and posits a reciprocity in the eschaton. Speaking of the Spirit and the Trinity, particularly the essence and the significance of the Spirit in the being of God and his activity in the world, he says, "This question is continually accompanied by the misleading presumption that it is entirely self-evident and not debatable that the work of the Spirit is simply to return us and our world to God. . . . Creation is not taken back, but redeemed, led forward, and brought to a consummation. The goal in all of this remains the same. It is that God—through the Messiah and the *Pneuma*—might eschatologically become all in all. In the eschaton, all that remains is the triune God and the naked existence of created things in their mutual opposition of reciprocal joy" (Van Ruler, *Calvinist Trinitarianism and Theocentric Politics,* 69, 71).

possibilities that may result from responding to common grace in various contexts? A positive response to these questions may orient those engaged in the public realm away from attempts to recover paradise and toward a land that is yet to come.

A second structural difference is between the category of substitution in Christology and reciprocity in pneumatology. Soteriologically, substitution is a category that describes Christ as the Messiah taking the place of sinners. Reciprocity refers to the activity of the Spirit not only "with" but also "together with" Christians.[6] In reciprocity, the Spirit's activity, rather than replacing that of humans, puts them to work. It speaks to the interaction between the individual Christian and the Spirit, resulting in not only awareness of the need for Christ but also conversion to Christ and subsequent life in Christ. Van Ruler highlights the distinction this way:

> In preaching we do not only proclaim accomplished divine decisions, decisions carried out in Christ. New divine decisions are also called for, decisions that are carried out in us. If we reflect on these matters in an exclusively christological way, we eventually arrive at a completely tyrannical position for the church and its preaching in the world. When we also think pneumatologically, we begin to realize that there is also a human juncture in the process of salvation. In the human heart as well as on Golgotha, a decision must be made.[7]

Reciprocity highlights human responsibility in salvation. In the realm of creation, the category of reciprocity may be helpful when considering the cooperation necessary for sociocultural engagement and development. Though common grace may exist through the command of Christ and the agency of the Spirit, development does not occur without human involvement. In other words, the ground will remain barren if left uncultivated. Though the Spirit enables development, the hands of humans are needed to till the garden of creation and yield the fruits of social development that comprise history. While it is not a relationship of give and take, the element of human responsibility is vital in the development of creation. The reciprocity between human responsibility and the Spirit's work in common grace is analogous to the relationship between individual Christians and the Spirit in sanctification, understood as a process.

6. Van Ruler, *Calvinist Trinitarianism and Theocentric Politics*, 34.
7. Ibid., 35.

As sanctification does not proceed without human response, neither does the public realm reflect the influence of divine ordinances on its structure if humans do not do the social-architectural work.

Third, Van Ruler distinguishes between the *eph hapax* (once for all) of Christ's atonement and the *eph hapax* of the outpouring of the Spirit. The significance of the outpouring is found in the fact that the Spirit remained on earth after Pentecost, in the church particularly.[8] Whereas there was descent and ascent in Christ's person and work, the Spirit's once-for-allness remains and provides continuity, "which is also found in the church, in its tradition, and in the historical, apostolic, mission activity."[9] For Van Ruler, this means that salvation fills and defines time. The kingdom of God is not restricted to Christ and the eschaton but is understood as a present reality. This leads to a comment that directly lends itself to further reflection on the Spirit's role in creation:

> We do not live purely in remembrance and expectation. The kingdom of God is not like a sea gull that—in the incarnation—swoops down and skims the surface of the water of temporal reality only to fly away and soar in the clouds until the *parousia*. The kingdom is a present reality. The kingdom does not only possess the form (*gestalte*) of the Messiah but also the form of the *Pneuma*. And the form of the *Pneuma* is more like the goal of the kingdom than the form of the Messiah. The focus is on us and our world. The goal is that we ourselves become images of God and experience this world as his kingdom.[10]

In terms of creation and common grace, Van Ruler's focus on the Spirit's remaining in creation is helpful yet requires an alteration. Though Van Ruler's third chapter notes that the Spirit has been present in creation since its inception,[11] his soteriological concerns lead him to highlight the unique indwelling of the Spirit post-Pentecost. For the purposes of creation and common grace, it is necessary to

8. Ibid., 38.
9. Ibid.
10. Ibid., 39.
11. "Because the indwelling of the Holy Spirit (*inhabitatio Spiritus Sancti*) is motivated by the entry of sin in the world, it must be distinguished from the creationally immanent activity of God the Spirit in the creature as such. The *inhabitatio* has its own distinct structure compared with this immanent activity (ibid., 56). My attempt at this point is to make such a distinction while positing a unique role of the Spirit in creation and common grace.

take a step back and note the uniqueness of the Spirit's immanence in creation. The following is implicit in Kuyper's description of the roles of Christ and the Spirit in creation.[12] While Christ arranged and subsequently upholds creation (a unique event and relationship), the Spirit's agency in common grace (or, to use Sinclair Ferguson's language, the Spirit's executive function) carries with it a once-for-all character by virtue of continual presence. This presence is characterized by sustaining life, restraining sin, and orienting creation to its *telos*. Van Ruler states that the Spirit does not skim the water's surface but remains present after Pentecost, and thus temporal reality is made significant. It is important to note, however, that the Spirit's presence since the beginning of creation serves as an affirmation of time and history even before the incarnation. Indeed, it can be said that the Spirit's work in creation, as distinct from Christ's work in forming creation, makes history possible by virtue of a teleological immanence.

Kuyper understood common grace as that which can and ought to direct attention to life in this world. The continual presence of the Spirit through common grace makes a focus on this world possible. In this way, *pneuma* takes form in the world, though in a nonsalvific way. If one goes along with Zuidema's resolution of the relationship Kuyper saw between particular grace and common grace, then it is possible to see how Kuyper's view of common grace is commensurate with Van Ruler's focus on the kingdom. Van Ruler focuses on the salvific, particular advent of the Spirit's outpouring, while Kuyper's view of the Spirit in creation speaks of the nonredemptive, common work of the Spirit. For Van Ruler, the Spirit enables Christians to experience the world as God's kingdom. With Kuyper (and Zuidema), one can say that it is possible to enable the kingdom to take form by responding to the possibilities in creation yielded by common grace. Those who wish to experience the kingdom can do so, but it requires a response to common grace that leads to a focus on this world and engagement in social-architectural development. To take such a view of kingdom-building does not require an eschatological commitment to postmillennialist forms, which require Christians to bring the kingdom of God to complete realization before Christ returns. In addition, a Constantinian triumphalism is not a necessary consequence of this response to common grace. The experience of

12. See Kuyper, *Work of the Holy Spirit*, 19–31, 43–47.

the kingdom made possible by common grace is a foretaste of the forthcoming consummation of the age. The *eph hapax* of the Spirit's nonredemptive immanence in creation is not altered by Pentecost except that the Spirit's particular work in salvation prompts potentially greater fidelity in response to common grace.[13]

Van Ruler's focus on the Spirit's continual immanence leads directly to his next structural difference, which is the category of indwelling. While indwelling is unacceptable christologically because of incarnational heresies such as Nestorianism, pneumatologically the category accurately describes the intimate union between God and humans. "God the Spirit, the triune God in the mode of the Spirit, dwells in and with us."[14] Van Ruler finds this category useful because it maintains the distinction between God and humans. In the third chapter, Van Ruler goes on to argue that indwelling is the central[15] and foundational category in pneumatology. In his soteriological perspective, the Spirit's work in and with Christians is the foundation for other categories such as reciprocity, imperfection, and an orientation to eschatology. Van Ruler states:

> The foundational idea (*grondgedachte*) in any completely valid pneu-matology can be summarized in the following proposition: the salvifi-cally directed indwelling of the Holy Spirit, who is God himself, in us, is the background of all activity of the Spirit in the present. In this particular formulation, that which is surprising and even alarming in the foundational idea of pneumatology comes properly and fully to expression. What is so surprising is that it is said of us that we are a dwelling place of God in the Spirit (Eph. 2:22). This mystery is perhaps even greater than that of God in Christ.[16]

The centrality of pneumatology in Van Ruler's thought forcefully appears in this statement. Of particular significance is his view that salvific indwelling is the foundation of all of the Spirit's activity in

---

13. It is also important to note that common grace, even when it is serving particular grace, is not to be used so that the church violates sphere sovereignty and directly attempts to shape and rule society. Particular grace enables Christians to recognize and appreciate the potential in the created order by virtue of common grace and then to engage the various arenas or spheres of society with the intent of glorifying God by developing those relatively independent spheres according to the divine ordinances.

14. Van Ruler, *Calvinist Trinitarianism and Theocentric Politics*, 39, 62.

15. Ibid., 50.

16. Ibid., 53.

the present. Clearly this contrasts with a focus on the Spirit's work in creation and common grace, in particular if this soteriologically focused indwelling is understood as foundational in a way that minimizes or engulfs the significance of the indwelling rooted in the *eph hapax* of the Spirit's teleological immanence in creation. Instead of stating that this salvific indwelling is the background for all of the Spirit's present activity, it may instead be suitable to state that the Spirit's continual immanence from the inception of creation is in fact the presupposition of all activity of the Spirit, past and present, and that the salvific indwelling is central and prominent, though carried out on the horizon of history that has existed since the inception of creation. Within the scope of time, the Spirit's common work in creation and history in this case becomes the background for the redemptive activity of the Spirit in its particular salvific indwelling. Because of the significance of salvation, the salvific indwelling is central to divine purposes, but it is not ultimately foundational for all of the Spirit's activity, as common grace does not become insignificant because of redemption.

"Indwelling" is a helpful way to speak of the Spirit's continual immanence in creation from its inception. As noted in the first chapter, indwelling language, or the use of alternatives, leads to Geiko Müller-Fahrenholz's pregnancy metaphor, Jürgen Moltmann's use of panentheism, and Mark Wallace's biocentric perspective as ways to describe the divine presence on earth and prompt better treatment of the world. Though helpful, these three earth-centered approaches run the risk of emphasizing immanence to the extent that the divine destiny is subjected to human faithfulness in caring for the environment.

If the category of indwelling stands, with the distinction between God and creation, as Van Ruler states, then there remains a way to emphasize immanence without the risk of moving toward identifying God with creation. Presence and inherence within creation need not become identity. Admittedly, this may seem to reduce the gravity involved in faithfully engaging creation, but it need not do so. It does bring to light the element of conflict, which Van Ruler points out. With his soteriological focus, he highlights the conflict between flesh and Spirit that will go on until the eschaton. In terms of creation and common grace, conflict may be understood as a matter of faithful or unfaithful response to common grace. Conflict arises when the possibilities given in common grace are ignored or misused, such as in the use of technological advances for diabolical purposes. An awareness of conflict highlights the risk involved in using the category of indwelling over the alternatives noted above. Nevertheless, conflict need not imply a fatalism that perceives only the worst uses of common grace. If the relatively conservative notion of indwelling is used to describe the Spirit's presence in creation, it is entirely possible that recognizing that "the world belongs to God" will not only engender respect for the biophysical world but also prompt a careful response to the cultural mandate. This concept of indwelling can lead to dominion that is not manifested as domination or destruction of the environment.

Of even greater interest is the fact that Van Ruler uses the category of indwelling to describe ways in which Christians are dwelling places of God in a corporate sense:

> Who is the "we" that is under discussion? One must not give too meagre an answer to this question. A proper answer spreads out in a fan-shaped way. The Spirit dwells in the church, in its institutional structures as well as in the mode of fellowship. But the Spirit also dwells in the Christian; in our body as well as in our heart as well, and in our inter-personal relationships. But the Spirit also dwells in nations and their cultures as they are taken up into the covenant with Israel by means of the spread of the apostolic Word. The Spirit dwells in the *corpus Christi,* in the *corpus Christiani,* and in the *corpus Christianum.*[17]

In expanding the notion of indwelling beyond individual Christians, Van Ruler clearly states that the Spirit can indwell nations and cultures. This follows from his earlier statement that the kingdom of God is present on earth. Yet he limits the Spirit's indwelling in nations and cultures to those that are under the covenant. It is as if the Spirit has this form of presence only where the kingdom of God has gained hegemony. In transposing this to creation and common grace, such a limited scope is not necessary.

17. Ibid., 40. In the third chapter, Van Ruler states it as follows: "In many respects the church is a communal reality. It is also a traditional reality. Tradition is the tradition of the Holy Spirit. Here again we need immediately to think through the entire breadth and abundance of the *Pneuma.* . . . : the nations of the earth, who in the course of the apostolic Word are incorporated into God's covenant with Israel, are also the dwelling place of God in the Spirit. The connectedness of the generations, the structure of society, the culture of these nations, the political formation of their life; all of this belongs essentially to the dwelling place of God in the world" (ibid., 54).

In contrast to Van Ruler's understanding of the Spirit's corporate indwelling, the perspective of creation and common grace leads to the inquiry, Where might the marks of the Spirit's work be found in nations and cultures that are not Christian? While Kuyper would certainly acknowledge that the Spirit indwells nations and cultures that relate to the covenant in some way, his perspective, such as on the arts, leads to the implication that the Spirit can indwell nations and cultures that are not self-consciously related to the covenant of Israel.

As shown in the previous chapter, Kuyper held that the Spirit, as a part of common grace, distributes gifts and talents of intellect and artistry to the regenerate and the unregenerate. As a result, it is possible to look upon the contributions of non-Christians in the arts and sciences and in the sociocultural arena with appreciation, though with a critical eye. A helpful term for this discussion is *civic righteousness*, which has been used[18] to speak of the fact that it is possible for non-Christians to perform civil good. Concerning such "righteousness" and the work of the Holy Spirit, John Bolt asks:

> If we can theologically conceive of the Holy Spirit giving the gift of life to an unbeliever and even further giving an unbeliever natural gifts (intelligence, musical ability, healthy and athletic body), why could we not conceive of a work of God the Holy Spirit that *providentially* influences an unbeliever's heart and will so that he or she does constructive and externally virtuous acts rather than destructive ones? What is the theological problem, for example, with suggesting that the Lord's anointed servant Cyrus's decree returning the Jews to their

18. This term was used in the "Third Point" of the 1924 Christian Reformed Church synodical pronouncement on common grace, which said, "Concerning the performance of so-called civic righteousness by the unregenerate, the Synod declares that according to Scripture and Confession the unregenerate, though incapable of any saving good (Canons of Dordt, III/IV, 3) can perform such civic good. This is evident from the quoted Scripture passages and from the Canons of Dordt, III, IV, 4, and the Belgic Confession, where it is taught that God, without renewing the heart, exercises such influence upon man that he is enabled to perform civic good; while it is evident from the quoted declarations of Reformed writers of the most flourishing period of Reformed theology, that our Reformed fathers from of old have championed this view." The entire text of all three points can be found in Herman Hoeksema, *The Protestant Reformed Churches in America: Their Origin, Early History, and Doctrine* (Grand Rapids: First Protestant Reformed Church, 1936), 84–85; and Cornelius Van Til, *Common Grace and the Gospel* (Phillipsburg, N.J.: Presbyterian & Reformed, 1972), 19–22. In addition, a recent article that addresses the term is John Bolt, "Common Grace, Theonomy, and Civic Good: The Temptations of Calvinist Politics," *Calvin Theological Journal* 33 (2000): 205–37.

homeland was providentially influenced by the Spirit of God? What is
the problem, particularly if we continue to insist that such deeds are
not at all "good" in the Catechism's sense but that the work of God's
Spirit is simply a means by which our Lord governs human history
and thus influences people to do acts of which he approves because
"they have reference to an end of which he [not only] approves" but
has in fact decreed?[19]

Bolt's inquiry relates the work of the Spirit in non-Christian acts of
civic righteousness to the greater work of God in bringing about the
fulfillment of the divine decrees. This opens a way to view not only
the deeds of individuals but also the social architecture of nations
and cultures as inhabited by the Spirit. Though various nations and
cultures may not be in the process of Christianization,[20] they play a
role, not readily or clearly perceivable at all times, in the fulfillment
of God's purpose for creation. Van Ruler makes a statement about
the hiddenness of the Spirit's work, which can be modified to the
work of the Spirit in creation. Van Ruler says, "The Spirit's activity,
in all its particularity, is *veiled (verhult)* in the ordinary, daily lives
and common forms of human existence."[21] We can expand this
statement to say that the Spirit's work, in its *common* activity, is
veiled in common forms of human existence and in the structure of
nations and cultures. As a result, it may be possible to say that the
Spirit indwells nations and cultures, though the reality of sin may
obfuscate the evidence of the Spirit in the deep structures of such
societies. With this orientation, it is also possible to encourage the
mining of other sociocultural systems for marks of the Spirit, leading
to the question, Is it possible to say that the Spirit is present, though
nonredemptively, wherever cultures and sociopolitical systems facilitate increasingly beneficial approaches to life in this world?[22] This

19. Bolt, "Common Grace, Theonomy, and Civic Good," 237.
20. Van Ruler actually uses the term *Christianization* when speaking of the Spirit's
indwelling and taking form in the nation and culture. Of great interest in this regard is
Van Ruler's observation that such formation varies in persons, nations, and cultures,
which suggests that there is not one particular form of cultural or natural life. See Van
Ruler, *Calvinist Trinitarianism and Theocentric Politics,* 42.
21. Ibid., 58. This statement is made in a section in which Van Ruler gives several
characteristics of the indwelling Spirit.
22. With a question such as this one, there is the subsequent question as to what
it is that constitutes a beneficial life. While such a question is ultimately beyond the
scope of this work, it can be said that Kuyper's perspective on a better life is found
in chap. 2.

investigation is not a form of engagement that uncritically accepts or approves of other systems, but it does provide a means for pursuing the discovery of creation ordinances that may not have been uncovered yet are evident in the attempts of non-Christians to construct and develop society. In this way, the category of indwelling[23] may be applied to the Spirit's work in creation and common grace and have broader use than in Van Ruler's work. The following section pursues in greater detail the question of "seeing" this work of the Spirit in culture.

Another structural difference is related to the category of perfection or infallibility. Van Ruler argues that while it is mandatory that one speak of Christ in a perfectionistic manner, "pneumatologically speaking, perfectionism is a life-threatening heresy. The Spirit can do a great deal and he does. The Christian and the church are divine realities. Sin and the demonic are confronted mightily. But the indwelling of the Spirit is carried out in a bitter and deadly conflict with the flesh."[24] Because pneumatology incorporates humanity, imperfection remains. This does not mean there is no transformation, but it does mean there is no final resolution to the conflict between the flesh and the Spirit until the eschaton.

This focus on imperfection raises an interesting point of reflection regarding the work of the Spirit in creation and common grace. The reality of imperfection in this life means that the various approaches to society and culture are never the exact representation or reflection of a world constructed according to the divine ordinances. When combined with the earlier category of reciprocity, this leads to the view that the engagement of the created order, no matter how faithfully intended, never fully transcends conflict in order to yield the ultimate social architecture. Though the conditions for life may be enhanced,

23. Herbert Richardson is another person who relates the idea of indwelling to pneumatology. In *Toward an American Theology*, he argues that the Holy Spirit fulfills God's chief purpose for creation (in answer to the question, "*Cur creatio?*") by indwelling the creation and ultimately sanctifying all things for the sake of God's glory. This is also a soteriologically focused approach but one that merits attention because of the centrality given to the category of indwelling. See Herbert W. Richardson, *Toward an American Theology* (New York: Harper & Row, 1967), 141–60.

24. Van Ruler, *Calvinist Trinitarianism and Theocentric Politics*, 43. In the third chapter, Van Ruler uses equally strong language, stating that "the idea of perfection is commanded christologically while it is forbidden pneumatologically. Whoever remains in Christ does not sin and is without guilt, but the Spirit does all his work in bitter conflict with the flesh" (*Calvinist Trinitarianism and Theocentric Politics*, 62–63).

the New Jerusalem is never achieved.[25] The category of imperfection is not to be understood as a disincentive for public engagement but as a catalyst for humility in the social-architectural task. It prompts continual refinement of the approach to public engagement and sociocultural development.

A final noteworthy structural difference comes as Van Ruler contrasts the orientation of Christology with that of pneumatology. While Christology focuses on Christ and the salvation rooted in him, pneumatology is oriented to the eternal kingdom and its glory.[26] Van Ruler argues that pneumatology should be understood more from the perspective of eschatology than from Christology and that the Spirit is more directly related to creation than to Christ. The reasoning for this structural difference is that the Spirit works in the lives of Christians and orients them toward the eternal future. This orientation focuses "on everything that is and everything that happens in creation and redemption, according to God's original and ultimate purposes."[27] If God's decrees, his ultimate purposes, are in view, then this orientation casts the gaze of Christians beyond an exclusive focus on salvation in Christ and toward the eternal kingdom. As mentioned above, a focus on the eternal kingdom actually leads to a focus on life in this world, for the eternal kingdom is already present. In his third chapter, Van Ruler elaborates on this by distinguishing the kingdom from the church:

25. Though he limits himself because of his soteriological focus, Van Ruler also gets at this idea in the third chapter through using the concept of plurality: "There are many salvation realities and many ways in which salvation is mediated. No single monistic principle exists which is capable of drawing them all together and from which they can all be deduced. In fact, there does not even exist a real hierarchy in which they can all be bound together in an above-and-below relationship. Here there is only a multiplicity and in this multiplicity only synthesis, a participation by which the one is grasped by, associates with, and above all, passes over into the other. To put it in other words: in the Spirit, there is no unity of being but a unity of love. To repeat: *this plurality of forms of the Spirit relativizes each of these forms and in this way preserves us from absolutizing them and from mistakenly anticipating the eschaton.* In summary: there exist God and humanity, the mediator and the Spirit, Scripture and tradition, proclamation and sacrament, ecclesiastical office (*ambt*) and the congregation (*gemeente*), the external and internal, church and state, redemption and creation" (ibid., 77–78, emphasis added). Though soteriology is Van Ruler's focus, his point about relativized forms is important when applied to church and state in his conception and to the results of social-architectural development in response to common grace in the case of the present work.

26. Ibid., 46.

27. Ibid., 46, 66–67.

We need to learn to experience the world as God experiences it or seeks to experience it through us. Is that the realization of the kingdom of God? The beginning of his kingdom? In any case, the kingdom of God is not limited to one of its forms (*gestalten*), the church. Life in the world is much more to be regarded as the kingdom of God than the church; at least its purpose is to become the kingdom of God. Furthermore, even the creation, the created reality, all that exists and that something indeed exists, is an anticipation of the eschaton.[28]

In addition, Van Ruler argues that terminology such as guarantee, sign, promise, and inheritance demonstrates the Spirit's orientation to the future.[29] This aspect of eschatological orientation can be helpful in a way similar to the category of adoption. The Spirit's teleological aspect encourages sociocultural development so that society in some sense bears the marks of the eternal kingdom. As noted in the discussion of imperfection, this engagement in the public realm demands an approach characterized by humility.

Van Ruler's third chapter, "Grammar of a Pneumatology," contains a relevant section that addresses a concern not raised in the chapter on structural differences. He directly asks, "What is pure humanity, social righteousness, political justice, a good deed? Are they immanent, historical magnitudes? Or are they also eschatological magnitudes? Is there a structure for creation, for the created and becoming reality, patterned by divine wisdom?"[30] Van Ruler answers that there is a pneumatological perspective from which to answer these concerns.

First, Van Ruler acknowledges the Spirit's work in creation in language similar to that of Kuyper. Calling the Spirit the principle of divine immanence in the created world, he says, "In the spring, no meadow or tree becomes green without the Spirit. All reality, created and upheld as it is, cannot exist apart from the Spirit."[31] The world, however, is also perceived as fallen and sinful. Nevertheless, it remains God's world and the arena for further acts of God.

Next, Van Ruler argues that God has an intended goal for life in the created world. The goal is achieved through the Spirit's entrance into existence so that ordinary forms of existence are raised to a higher

28. Ibid., 67.
29. Ibid., 66–67.
30. Ibid., 84.
31. Ibid.

level, though not to perfection. At this point it is important to highlight Van Ruler's soteriological focus. It is through the Spirit's salvific work that such elevation occurs. As argued above, such elevation occurs as much through the possibilities of common grace as through particular grace. Van Ruler moves on to argue that the Spirit's use of the concrete givens of humanity and culture extends to "corrupt and lost reality."[32] Stating that God is not reluctant to sully his hands, Van Ruler suggests that the Spirit reaches out and brings humanity and culture back to its proper being by means of regeneration and conversion. Then comes a most interesting comment: "Apart from Christ and the Spirit, apart from God, culture and the state are not genuine possibilities."[33] This leads Van Ruler to conclude that the answer to the question posed is rooted in the presuppositions of the Christian faith. To have the best society, the Spirit must imprint the form of Christ on all reality, including humanity and culture.[34] "A 'dogmatically determined' cultural synthesis is, therefore, not only an absolute necessity for the Christian church, but also a necessary condition for a lasting culture."[35]

For Van Ruler, the Spirit can yield improvements in society and culture only as a part of the process of redemption. If one contends that common grace is a reality, then such limitations do not exist. It is possible, even in nations and cultures foreign to the covenant, to find evidence of the Spirit's work in common grace.

The interaction with Van Ruler has led to the use of categories such as continuous creation, reciprocity, an *eph hapax* of continual immanence, indwelling, imperfection, and eschatological orientation as ways to understand the work of the Spirit in creation and common grace. In pursuing such categories, it is possible to articulate the Spirit's work in terms that can be considered pneumatological. While such terms may have application to Christology, they have pneumatological nuances and, more importantly, significance for a focus on creation and history. With this pneumatological perspective, the Spirit's work is understood in a more fully trinitarian fashion. The Third Person of the Godhead becomes perceived more accurately as an equal member when greater light is shed on a category such as indwelling. In addition, this perspective helps to highlight the non-

32. Ibid., 85–86.
33. Ibid., 86.
34. Ibid.
35. Ibid.

redemptive work of the Spirit, addressing in some sense the concerns raised in chapter 1. Before turning to the approach to public theology derived from this pneumatological perspective, we must consider how it is possible to detect the work of the Spirit in culture and society.

The Spirit in Culture and Society: How Do We "See" It?

If the Spirit indwells nations and cultures by virtue of continual immanence, how is it possible to discern the "marks" of the Spirit in their cultural and social lives? Another way to phrase the question in light of common grace is, How do we know that a development in society or culture is a fruit of common grace?

A helpful scriptural text for this inquiry is Philippians 4:8 (NIV):

> Finally, brothers, whatever is true, whatever is noble, whatever is right, whatever is pure, whatever is lovely, whatever is admirable—if anything is excellent or praiseworthy—think about such things.

In this text, Paul encourages his readers to acknowledge the good things that exist in the non-Christian world. While he has urged the Philippians to be distinctive in their behavior, he also urges them not to regard the good things in society and culture with disdain.

This chapter has argued that the good things that exist in society and culture are a result of the Spirit's continual immanence in creation. By way of direct application to our subject, how do we respond to Paul's encouragement to recognize and appreciate the fruits of common grace? Stanley Grenz, Clark Pinnock, and Amos Yong have undertaken this question, and a brief overview of their perspectives may help us take steps toward answering this question.

Most recently, Stanley Grenz has addressed the relationship between the Spirit and culture in *Beyond Foundationalism*, coauthored with John R. Franke.[36] While his focus is on the role of culture as a theological source, Grenz's observations about the relationship between the Spirit and culture are directly relevant to the present inquiry. Specifically, Grenz states that the Spirit's speaking through

---

36. Stanley Grenz and John R. Franke, *Beyond Foundationalism* (Louisville: Westminster John Knox, 2001). Grenz has also addressed this topic in other texts such as *Revisioning Evangelical Theology: A Fresh Agenda for the Twenty-first Century* (Downers Grove, Ill.: InterVarsity, 1993); and *Renewing the Center: Evangelical Theology in a Post-theological Era* (Grand Rapids: Baker, 2000).

culture is related to the fact that the Spirit's speaking through Scripture is always contextual:

> It always comes to its hearers within a specific historical-cultural context. Of course, throughout church history the Spirit's ongoing provision of guidance has always come, and now continues to come, as the community of Christ as a specific people in a specific setting hears the Spirit's voice speaking in the particularity of its historical-cultural context. . . . The specificity of the Spirit's speaking means that the conversation with culture and cultural context is crucial to the hermeneutical task. We seek to listen through scripture to the voice of the Spirit, who speaks to us in the particularity of the historical-cultural context in which we live.[37]

A part of the hermeneutical process is interaction with the discoveries and insights that arise in various disciplines of human learning. These discoveries and insights, Grenz argues, inform our theological construction because they are perceived to be truth, which ultimately comes from God. More specifically, the pneumatological basis for perceiving the Spirit's voice in culture is rooted in the belief that all creaturely life flourishes as a result of the Spirit's role as the life-giving power of creation:

> Because the life-giving Creator Spirit is present wherever life flourishes, the Spirit's voice can conceivably resound through many media, including the media of human culture. Because Spirit-induced human flourishing evokes cultural expression, we can anticipate in such expressions traces of the Creator Spirit's presence. Consequently, we should listen intently for the voice of the Spirit, who is present in all life and therefore who "precedes" us into the world, bubbling to the surface through the artifacts and symbols humans construct.[38]

The impetus to "read" the signs of the Spirit in culture is not a reason to set Scripture and culture against each other. The primacy of the text remains, and it serves as a canon for hearing and evaluating the signs of the Spirit in culture. From Grenz's perspective, these two forms of speaking work together in one moment of communication. "We listen for the voice of the Spirit who speaks the Word through

37. Grenz and Franke, *Beyond Foundationalism*, 161.
38. Ibid., 162.

the word within the particularity of the hearer's context, and who thereby can speak in all things."[39]

In light of the intended aims of his text, it is not surprising that Grenz does not seek to articulate the implications of his view of the Spirit and culture for public theology. Nevertheless, his conclusions lead to the view that evidence of the Spirit can be found in the world outside the church, though in his approach such evidence can be detected only in concert with the task of reading and interpreting Scripture in the Christian community.

Pinnock addresses the issue while seeking to discern the truth among the cacophony and ambiguity of the claims of the various world religions. While acknowledging the universal presence of the Spirit, Pinnock resists identifying the Spirit with everything in the world, particularly with things that are deceptive and destructive, such as the "progressive" societies of Nazi Germany and Mao's China. These societies appeared to promote great new possibilities for a flourishing humanity but proved to be oppressive. In light of the potential for such deception, one must test the spirits to see if they are truly "of the Spirit."

The criterion for discernment is linked to Christology. In light of the link between the work of Christ and the work of the Spirit, we must search for truth incarnate. The Spirit agrees with the Son's words and actions. John 14:26 and 16:13–14 reveal that the Spirit will speak only in accordance with the Son, leading Pinnock to conclude that incarnate wisdom is the criterion. "What the Spirit says and does cannot be opposed to revelation in Christ, because Spirit is bound to the Word of God. The reciprocity is clear—Spirit births the Son in Mary's womb, and the Son identifies the ways of the Spirit. To identify prevenience, we look for the fruit of the Spirit and for the way of Jesus Christ."[40] More specifically, Pinnock argues that the pattern found in the Gospel narratives aids discernment of the Spirit's movement:

> So wherever we see traces of Jesus in the world and people opening up to his ideals, we know we are in the presence of the Spirit. Wherever, for

39. Ibid., 163.

40. Clark Pinnock, *Flame of Love: A Theology of the Holy Spirit* (Downers Grove, Ill.: InterVarsity, 1997), 209. It is notable that Pinnock uses the term *prevenience*, as this reveals Arminian sympathies that express the common work of the Spirit as potentially preparatory for salvation, as opposed to the nonredemptive conception of common grace in the present work.

example, we find self-sacrificing love, care about community, longings for justice, wherever people love one another, care for the sick, make peace not war, wherever there is beauty and concord, generosity and forgiveness, the cup of cold water, we know the Spirit of Jesus is present.[41]

Pinnock hastens to add that such evidence of the Spirit is detectable in actions and good works that reflect the kingdom. The fruit of the Spirit should be discerned not only by investigating propositional truth but also by evidence of transformed life. While the latter reflects Pinnock's inquiry concerning the truth that is available through other religions, his christological approach also serves the effort to discern the evidence of the Spirit in culture and society generally. Because of his primary focus, Pinnock, like Grenz, does not develop the implications of his perspective for public theology.

Amos Yong's *Beyond the Impasse: Toward a Pneumatological Theology of Religions* specifically attempts to provide an approach for discerning the work of the Spirit in the world. Like Pinnock, Yong is concerned with world religions but addresses the issue of discernment more broadly. Yong finds that Scripture speaks of two kinds of discernment: the spiritual gift of discerning spirits and a broader discernment that requires the cultivation and exercise of human perceptual abilities. Both kinds require dependence on the Spirit. The task of the latter approach to discernment comes to everyone and is most germane to this discussion.

For Yong, the task of discernment, with or without the spiritual gift, is to examine the phenomenal features of things in order to discover their inner aspect. "One proceeds to the task of spiritual discernment only by concentrating on what is phenomenologically revealed to the broad range of human senses. In short, only sensitive observation of

41. Ibid., 209–10. Here Pinnock sounds similar to Kuyper on the effects of common grace, though Kuyper is more effusive and speaks of technological and institutional progress: "One common grace aims at the *interior,* the other at the *exterior* part of our existence. The former is operative wherever civic virtue, a sense of domesticity, natural love, the practice of human virtue, the improvement of the public conscience, integrity, mutual loyalty among people, and a feeling for piety leaven life. The latter is in evidence when human power over nature increases, when invention upon invention enriches life, when international communication is improved, the arts flourish, the sciences increase our understanding, the conveniences and joys of life become more vital and radiant, forms become more refined, and the general image of life becomes more winsome" (Abraham Kuyper, "Common Grace," in *Abraham Kuyper: A Centennial Reader,* ed. James D. Bratt [Grand Rapids: Eerdmans, 1998], 181).

the behaviors and manifestations of the thing in question enables one to pierce through its outer forms into its inner habits, dispositions, tendencies, and powers."[42] This process of discernment is a dynamic process that requires time, and the criteria of discernment need to pertain to the object in question. Yong states, "It would be appropriate, for example, to apply moral and religious criteria to adult persons and religious organizations, less appropriate to apply the same criteria to teenagers or environmental groups, and completely inappropriate to apply them to infants or the work of mathematicians. . . . In short, discernment is particularistic in nature, focused on specific actualities and assessing such according to the norms and criteria appropriate to them."[43]

How does one assess whether something is of the Spirit or even of the demonic? Yong argues that the objective is to sort out whether the subject or the object in question is fulfilling its divinely appointed reasons for being. The extent to which something radically departs from its purpose and function and has destructive effects in its relationships reveals whether something may be characterized as demonic. In making assessments, Yong also states that biblical norms are required, though this also requires wisdom, since both Scripture and the world need to be read accurately to apply such norms. The process of discernment is complex, and Yong urges us to recognize that all our criteriologies should be recognized as human constructions, "our best efforts to discern the Spirit of God from the demonic in our world of flux—even as we attempt to faithfully rely upon, listen to, and follow the Spirit."[44] Some ambiguity will attend our efforts at discernment because we can only partially glimpse the spiritual world through an examination of the material world. As a result, conclusive articulations will be hard to come by. As with Grenz and Pinnock, Yong does not address issues of public theology, but the mode of discernment he presents has applicability to everything in the world, from the religious to the artistic to the political.

In their acknowledgment that evidence of the Spirit's work can be found in cultural production and incarnate truth, Grenz and Pinnock affirm this chapter's contention that the continual immanence of the Spirit may be reflected in noncovenantal nations and cultures. While reading cultural signs along with Scripture in the community

42. Amos Yong, *Beyond the Impasse: Toward a Pneumatological Theology of Religions* (Grand Rapids: Baker Academic, 2002), 151.
43. Ibid., 157.
44. Ibid., 159.

and observing patterns consonant with the gospel are helpful tools of discernment, they yield limited assistance in our search for the implications for public theology. Yong takes us further by prompting us to examine carefully the phenomena found in societies and cultures. His proposal prompts us to inquire about the purpose and function of cultures and governments and to develop criteria specific to the object of inquiry, all the while being aware of the provisional nature of our conclusions. Though questions more specific to public theology remain, Yong offers a valuable contribution.

What kinds of public theology questions remain? Here we might ask about cultural developments and forms of society that seem to promote human flourishing yet have no explicit parallel in Scripture. For example, in what way might technological developments be seen as a fruit of common grace if they enhance human possibilities for self-determination? How do we assess seemingly "neutral" developments that could harm as much as help human life depending on the application? How do we discern whether approaches to leadership, governance, and economic life spring from common grace? We are helped by inquiring into the purpose and functions of culture and government, but how do we answer such questions in diverse civilizations? Should all nations be aiming for the same kind of culture and government? As a specific example, should all nations ultimately function as a kind of democracy with particular forms of cultural expression in art, music, and architecture?

In tandem with Yong's emphasis on the provisionality of judgments in the ongoing task of discernment, an aspect of the doctrine of providence could be helpful. Providence turns our attention to God's care for creation through preservation and sustenance directed toward God's purposes.[45] Yong's proposal leads us to consider the extent to which a culture or government is fulfilling its divinely given purpose. Providence reminds us of God's involvement in history and the fact that God will ultimately direct all things toward their purpose in the fulfillment of his redemptive plan. This reminder from providence sharpens our focus in the sense that we inquire into the purpose and function of things not merely according to the norms particular to the area of inquiry but also in light of where a particular

---

45. Among many, three helpful treatments on providence are G. C. Berkouwer, *The Providence of God* (Grand Rapids: Eerdmans, 1952); Benjamin Wirt Farley, *The Providence of God* (Grand Rapids: Baker, 1988); and Paul Helm, *The Providence of God* (Downers Grove, Ill.: InterVarsity, 1994).

development may fit into God's overarching plan. With this in mind, judgments can be only provisional, but the frustrations that attend the process of discernment are tempered by hope rooted in God's providential activity. Throughout the ongoing task of discernment, we depend on the Spirit, who both providentially sustains creation through common grace and enables us to glimpse his work in the world that manifests the fruit of the same grace.

Where does this leave us? At the very least, we can examine the phenomena of cultures and societies for the fruits of common grace and judge them according to their clear alignment with biblical and particularly christological norms while also asking questions concerning the role a given culture or society plays in the scheme of divine providence. The provisionality of judgments should make us cautious about making definitive pronouncements that a particular cultural or political development has come from the Spirit, as if a form of cultural life or government were messianic. In fact, a lesson to learn from the previous century is that "progress" can lead to genocides and world wars as much as it can yield beneficial revolutions in medicine and communications. Instead of triumphantly identifying developments as "of the Spirit," we should cautiously undertake the process of discernment and humbly offer the results of our discovery.

Furthermore, evaluations of cultural and political developments should be attended by the consideration that they could be fruit of common grace for a particular point in time in the development of a society. Considering any development a manifestation of the ultimate cultural or political *telos* for a society only reflects hasty judgment and a hubris born of amnesia concerning our limited vision. With Yong, we should view discerning the work of the Spirit as an ongoing, dynamic discipline of the Christian life. With this cautious approach, we can make tentative pronouncements about whether we have observed the fruit of common grace and over time refine our judgments as we see whether cultural or political life is increasing or decreasing in accordance with God's purposes.

PUBLIC THEOLOGY AND THE STEWARDSHIP OF CREATION

The work of the Holy Spirit in creation is characterized by the central category of indwelling. The Spirit's inherence in creation has been constant from the inception of creation and has enabled not only the preservation and survival of life but also the development of life culturally and socially. Though sin is a reality, the Spirit's indwelling presence resists the dissolution of the biophysical order and orients the development of history toward its ultimate eschatological goal. As Kuyper argued, the Spirit leads creation to its destiny, the glory of God. Humans play a vital role in leading creation to its *telos,* and their efforts at social-architectural planning and development reveal the reciprocity inherent in common grace. At the same time, the results of society building reflect the imperfection that always results because of the limitations of those who would strive to improve the character of human life in the realms of society and culture. Though the ordinances of creation are discovered, refined, and maybe re-created, no society approximates the eschatological kingdom. Though the various attempts to develop society are relativized by human limitations, it may be possible to detect (provisionally) evidence of the Spirit's work in various cultures and nations, even those that are outside the covenant and not in the process of Christianization.

What kind of public theology emerges as a result of this attempt to update Kuyper's view of the Spirit's work in creation? The Spirit's work in creation leads to a public theology construed as the "responsible"[46] stewardship of creation. Based on Kuyper, the Spirit's work in making common grace available through indwelling presence (and the subsequent categories) leads to an approach to creation conceived as a wide-ranging form of stewardship.

How does this pneumatologically derived approach to creation stewardship relate to the contemporary situation? In an interesting reversal of a widespread consensus, many consider stewardship a patronizing approach that permits humanity to act destructively in regard to the environment. James Nash expresses the dilemma well:

> Though the ethical concept of stewardship justifiably has positive connotations to many Christians, implying love and service, it has negative ones for substantial numbers of environmentalists (including many Christians). Stewardship conveys to them, because of historical associations with Gifford Pinchot and others in this century, the notion

46. The term *responsible,* while implied in the notion of stewardship, is necessary in this case because an approach of stewardship will not necessarily be responsible. Bad stewardship is as possible as responsible stewardship.

of anthropocentric and instrumental management of the biosphere as humanly owned "property" and "resources."[47]

Nash is ambivalent toward the use of the term and understandably so. Nevertheless, misappropriation of the stewardship paradigm does not necessarily require lexical or conceptual alternatives. Rather, a proper application of stewardship is needed that provides a counterbalance to the caricatured representations of the paradigm in many circles. In this regard, while it is proper to express concern that the exercise of human management of the resources of creation may lead to a *telos* of entropy rather than fruitful development, this happens only when ideological conceptions rule that deny the radical sovereignty of God and the cultural mandate.

The Spirit's work in creation and common grace leads to a call for responsible stewardship by virtue of the intimate relationship between the Spirit and creation through the indwelling presence. Because of the Spirit's role in common grace, all persons are called to greater responsibility as stewards of creation. The recipients of particular grace have a greater motive for heeding the call to responsible stewardship, but common grace provides even the unregenerate with some capacity for developing creation to the glory of God.[48]

How does the Spirit's work in creation and common grace lead to a level of responsible stewardship in which nature is respected rather than viewed as the object of simple anthropocentric domination? While this book, with Kuyper, holds to a view of "dominion" in which the world is subject to humanity, it also sees the human race as subject to the God whom we rightly know in Jesus Christ. Thus, this subjection is understood through the perspective of the loving lordship of Christ, which is far from abusive. The exercise of dominion is a "holy duty" to be performed under God in all the world in all parts of life.[49] In the performance of this duty, "Christian action in the domain of common grace must minister to the structures of creation and the structures of common grace (which for all intents

47. James A. Nash, *Loving Nature: Ecological Integrity and Christian Responsibility* (Nashville: Abingdon, 1991), 107.
48. S. U. Zuidema, "Common Grace and Christian Action in Abraham Kuyper," in *Communication and Confrontation,* ed. Gerben Groenewoud, trans. Harry Van Dyke (Toronto: Wedge, 1972), 65.
49. Abraham Kuyper, *Calvinism: Six Lectures Delivered in the Theological Seminary at Princeton* (New York: Revell, 1899), 31.

and purposes coincide)—instead of overturning them! . . . Its results can only be a higher development of 'nature' and the 'natural,' i.e., of the creature."[50] Nature is lifted and respected in an appropriate, "responsible" response to common grace. This leads to an urge for cooperation with the Spirit in helping creation reach its potential. Creation is affirmed as good and worthy of full, responsible engagement, and life in this world is perceived positively. To briefly return to the garden metaphor, one can say that tilling the garden of creation should be an act of joyful reciprocity.

Furthermore, because of common grace, "no Christian has a legitimate reason for withdrawing from the world of God's creating. That holds for the whole of creation, to its farthest reaches; that holds for 'all areas'; that holds in principle for the whole world of culture, politics included."[51] There is no room for a sectarian apoliticism in Kuyper's pneumatology nor for an anti-creational opposition between technology and theology. Rather, science and politics become means of respecting creation as they are transformed in a stewardly fashion to the glory of God. This kind of approach could address Moltmann's concerns about a mechanistic worldview that leads to destructive domination of the biophysical order.[52]

This pneumatologically derived approach to stewardship leads to a positive environmental perspective and to well-considered approaches to the environment without the need to resort to alternative proposals. As noted above in the discussion of indwelling, conceptually, it is not necessary to conceive of the God/world or Spirit/world relation in pantheistic or panentheistic forms to produce or encourage sound ecological theology and public policy. The many ideological avenues that emphasize God's immanence in order to raise or create ecological consciousness run the risk of attributing the negative as well as the positive aspects of the world to God, including evil and injustice.[53] Also, these conceptual paradigms, when taken to the extreme, put God at risk by connecting the destiny of creation with divine destiny.

50. Zuidema, "Common Grace and Christian Action in Abraham Kuyper," 72.
51. Ibid.
52. See chap. 1.
53. Admittedly, some might argue that Reformed Christians of a strong supralapsarian tendency are guilty of the same association, as everything that occurs ultimately serves God's purposes in bringing himself glory through the salvation of the elect and the reprobation of the nonelect. See Richard Mouw, *He Shines in All That's Fair: Culture and Common Grace* (Grand Rapids: Eerdmans, 2001), 36, 58–59, 61–63.

While Scripture affirms that God responds to human action in creation, and even that God grieves over sin, it does not portray a "God at risk" who is somehow at the mercy of human decision. Is it not more accurate to conceive of God as Kuyper does, as a transcendent trinitarian God who relates to creation in an intimate manner through the indwelling, sustaining presence of the Spirit?

Practically speaking, responsible stewardship may manifest itself in environmental concern that leads to various forms of social action. There is no place for callous disregard of the environment because of an otherworldly focus. Indeed, there has been much Christian neglect of the environment, and the time is now at hand to develop an orthopraxis that reflects the high ideals of responsible stewardship.[54] To do nothing is to resist the Spirit and misuse common grace.

While it is easy to see how the Kuyper-based view of the Spirit's work in creation leads to responsible ecological stewardship, how is it that the Spirit's involvement in creation leads to responsible cultural development and political involvement? How is it that the Spirit's indwelling, life-giving, and sustaining presence in creation prompts a response to the cultural mandate? A good way to understand this relation is through inquiring into the function of culture and politics. If we understand both politics and culture as activities in which we "work with" the material of creation or "act on" creation, then it follows that both areas require responsible stewardship. The development and transformation of the potential in nature by drawing nature into the realm of human care is the domain of creation stewardship.

As with the environment, it is important to apply the political and cultural forms of action born of responsible stewardship to the created order. We must not understand stewardship and dominion as license for domination. As S. U. Zuidema states, all activity in creation, the realm of common grace, must minister to the structures of creation. Culturally speaking, the objective is to develop human potentialities and sociocultural structures toward a God-glorifying end. Matters such as art and technology are facets of a divine commission. Zuidema puts it best in regard to politics: "Christian political action will have to be more than lobbying for legislation to preserve the 'Christian heritage' of Sunday observance: it will have to be the expression of a political philosophy and program that touches upon every aspect

54. In this regard, see Calvin B. DeWitt, *Caring for Creation: Responsible Stewardship of God's Handiwork* (Grand Rapids: Baker, 1998).

of political life."[55] Kuyper's objective in regard to common grace was not for Christians to be a certain breed of citizen but for them to be simply citizens par excellence who embody the best in public and private life.[56] As stated earlier, Kuyper primarily had Christians in mind, for those who are being sanctified will be most concerned to be good stewards of common grace. However, this does not mean that non-Christians are unable to develop creation, though they will be less inclined toward cultivating the potencies in common grace for the purposes of God's glory. Yet in spite of the lack of a regenerate heart, it is still possible for the gifts of common grace to be used and developed in a way that bears marks of the Spirit. As argued above, even in persons, nations, and cultures that are not under the covenant, the Spirit's work in common grace may be in evidence, even if it is unacknowledged by those engaged in the tasks of cultural and political development.

This discussion of the Spirit as the ultimate driving force behind ecological, political, and cultural responsibility eventually leads to the question of appearances. What forms will ecological plans, political philosophies, or cultural norms and values take if there is true reciprocity and cooperation with the Spirit's enabling, sustaining, and developing power? What should this cooperation look like? Should it look like Calvin's Geneva mediated through Kuyper's Amsterdam? Hardly, for the contemporary context is not identical to either era and has its own unique opportunities and challenges. Some may desire a return to an imagined sociocultural paradise of a bygone era, and others may desire the perpetuation of the status quo. Then it is good to heed Van Ruler's words concerning the relativization of forms, Yong's emphasis on provisionality, and these words from Nicholas Wolterstorff regarding his qualified admiration of Calvinism: "that most insufferable of all human beings, the triumphalist Calvinist, the one who believes that the revolution instituting the holy commonwealth has already occurred and that his or her task is now simply to keep it in place. Of these triumphalist Calvinists the United

---

55. Zuidema, "Common Grace and Christian Action in Abraham Kuyper," 73.

56. Ibid. It is also important to note Kuyper's discussions of multiformity, which though applied to ecclesiology and doctrine are also applicable to forms of national and cultural life. Though Kuyper had definite opinions about what constituted the best culture, he also respected different approaches to politics and culture. See Kuyper, *Calvinism,* 78; and Abraham Kuyper, *Principles of Sacred Theology* (Grand Rapids: Eerdmans, 1954), 295.

States and Holland have both had their share."[57] It is also important to attend to the cautious words of Richard Mouw:

> Those of us who endorse the idea of common grace would do well to recognize the ways in which its teachings frequently have fostered a triumphalist spirit that has encouraged false hopes for a premature transformation of sinful culture. But for all that, the theologians of common grace have nonetheless been right to insist that the God who is unfolding his multiple purposes in this present age also calls his people to be agents of those diverse Kingdom goals. It is important for us in these difficult days to cultivate an appropriate Calvinist sense of modesty and humility in our efforts at cultural faithfulness. But we cannot give up on the important task—which the theologians of common grace have correctly urged upon us—of actively working to discern God's complex designs in the midst of our deeply wounded world.[58]

These words fall into line with Kuyper's desire to be mindful of the need to update not only theology but also the social and cultural approaches to society according to the needs of the day. As opposed to the hubris of the triumphalist who is content with the status quo, responsible stewardship requires a posture of humility. Rather than believing that the kingdom has come in a particular society, it is important to remember that every society is still moving toward the ultimate *telos,* and none is close to the perfect reflection of the new earth of the eschaton. Mouw's words also point to the teleological thrust of the indwelling Spirit. The impulse for development leads to social and cultural worlds not yet seen, though all will be imperfect until the final re-creation. This sentiment also applies when considering the fruits of progress. With Cornelis van der Kooi, it is important to be cautious, but it is also important to press forward, though with sobriety. The sense in which the motives of Kuyper and Calvin are worthy of emulation is in the commitment to discernment in the social-architectural task. We, like they, need to discern where the works of responsible stewardship lie in the natural and cultural cities of our day.[59]

57. Nicholas Wolterstorff, *Until Justice and Peace Embrace* (Grand Rapids: Eerdmans, 1983), 21.

58. Mouw, *He Shines in All That's Fair,* 50.

59. This form of discernment differs from examining cultures to see if they contain the fruit of common grace. Discernment here relates to choosing the appropriate areas for the application of stewardship and the cultivation of creation so that the fruit of common grace may emerge.

Another question raised is this: Is it necessary for one to ally one-self with Kuyper's political and cultural program, in which he called for separate Christian organizations? Or one may ask the opposite question: Are there arenas of cultural life in which common grace demands cooperation or even alliance with those who are not Christian? In both instances, the answer is possibly, but one cannot make hard-and-fast assertions concerning ancillary particulars, since they may vary among societies and cultures.

One answer to the question of social forms is that, while not rigidly calling for a specifically Christian, universally applicable type of ecology, politics, and culture, there should be certain common characteristics among all attempts to be responsible stewards of creation. What are these characteristics? At the very least, there should be a climate of service and nurture, a climate of justice, an attitude of humility, and a zeal for creative development—characteristics that are encouraged by common grace. Regarding the latter two questions, it is certainly not necessary to become Kuyperian clones. For example, while in some cases it is indeed necessary for Christians to form separate organizations, and while some social structures may even call for the manifestation of the church militant, all societies are not the same, and the requirements of responsible stewardship will vary, even to the inclusion of situations in which Christians work with non-Christians. In fact, it is practically impossible to participate effectively in a modern democracy without some alliance with those of different beliefs. Moreover, although there is value in the common grace paradigm, we do not necessarily have to follow Kuyper's application of that paradigm (or that of his followers). One may agree with Kuyper's political and cultural views to various degrees, yet one need not adopt his positions in order to appreciate, utilize, and develop his work.

At this point, it is significant to present a particular point that Richard Mouw addresses in his recent work on common grace. In line with Zuidema's sentiment, Mouw speaks of "common grace ministries" to describe cultural engagement. While encouraging political activity, Mouw, inspired by Kuyper,[60] extends the response to common grace to every area of life and speaks of ministries not often considered in discussions of common grace:

60. Mouw, *He Shines in All That's Fair*, 81.

The Christian psychologist who encourages her non-Christian clients to honor commitments, the Christian literature professor at a secular university who highlights themes in a novel that celebrate faithfulness and telling the truth, the Christian corporate manager who instills the will to serve in employees, the Christian farmer who employs specific agricultural methods that demonstrate respect for the integrity of the creation—all of these promote the goodness associated with common grace. We should not confine our attention, then, to how unbelievers on occasion perform those deeds that better the lot of other human beings. We should also think about the ways in which we ourselves, in performing righteous acts that affect the lives of unbelievers, can promote the gifts of common grace.[61]

Mouw's intent is to highlight the broad ways in which a response to common grace can be observed and emulated. His examples typify an approach of responsible stewardship over creation. The use of the term *ministry* is important and strategic for the conception of stewardship of creation rooted in common grace. If public theology is understood as a kind of ministry, then it could possibly facilitate fruitful discussion with those who perceive of stewardship as the destructive domination of the created order. In addition, it contributes to the posture of humility that Mouw encourages when responding to common grace and engaging in social-architectural activity.

The second point Mouw makes is that the approach of common grace is not devoid of theological messiness. He states:

As Calvinists, we must seek the common good with the clear awareness that in the public square we are surrounded by people "who call good evil and evil good, who put darkness for light and light for darkness, who put bitter for sweet and sweet for bitter" (Isaiah 5:20). And yet it is in these circumstances that we hear again the Lord's ancient call to his redeemed people to seek the welfare of the city of our exile. This messiness, then, isn't something that we can hope to eliminate; nor can we minimize it as we develop our strategies for public witness. To endorse a common grace theology is to learn to live with some theological messiness. This ought not to trouble Calvinists, for whom the experience of theological messiness should be a healthy reminder of the ways in which all of our theological probings will eventually bring us to humble acknowledgment of the divine mysteries.[62]

61. Ibid., 81–82.
62. Ibid., 87.

Theological messiness, like the pneumatological category of imperfection, is not a disincentive for the tasks of theology and cultural engagement but rather a constant reminder of the need for humility. It is in this sense that Mouw goes on to caution the proponents of common grace concerning the way to read the contributions of non-Christian persons and, by implication, the social architecture of non-Christian nations and cultures. Mouw urges his readers to evaluate ideas and attempts at social improvement in a way that neither uncritically accepts nor dismisses the object of observation as bearing marks of the Spirit.[63] Wrestling with the reality of common grace requires continual refinement in understanding and continual revision of attempts at a coherent presentation of a Spirit-based reality that prompts responsible stewardship.

Pneumatologically derived responsible stewardship provides an impetus and a rationale for engagement with the myriad, complex issues that impact society. It is important to recover a proper understanding and application of the stewardship paradigm, and a Kuyper-based approach can be helpful. In seeking to complete the picture of the Spirit's role in creation and the vital implications that follow, one could do far worse than to incorporate the essence of Kuyper's approach. The Spirit's sustaining and developing power rouses us from our neglect of the environment and our lack of substantive progress in political and cultural development. If this "call of the Spirit" is heeded, then the stage may be set for significant, transformative contributions to the issues of the day.

63. Ibid., 93.

5

COMPELLED TO "GO PUBLIC"

THE STORY THUS FAR

In this work, the discipline of systematic theology exhibits the convergence of the themes of creation and history, cosmic pneumatology, and public theology. Abraham Kuyper was a public theology incarnate, for he practiced a form of public engagement catalyzed by common grace, which is brought about by the Spirit's work in creation. Though common grace and pneumatology are the central foci here, it is also important to recall the significance of Kuyper's strong focus on the sovereignty of God, in particular when considering the ultimate foundation for his approach to public theology. Without this doctrine of sovereignty, there can be no emphasis on the ordinances of creation or the sovereignty of the spheres in society. In addition, it is important to recall that Kuyper's supralapsarian view caused problems for his doctrine of common grace and that the infralapsarian insights of Richard Mouw provide a perspective that allows common and particular grace to have distinct purposes.

The themes of creation and history help to distinguish this work from other texts that emphasize the doctrine of creation. By understanding history as the human activity on the horizon of the biophysical order, it is possible to speak of a theology of creation that does not have causality as its primary concern. Within Kuyper's work, common grace, the nonsalvific grace of God, serves as the precondition for history, for without such grace, human development and engagement with the material of creation are not possible. Though this book does not prominently highlight this distinctive emphasis on the doctrine of creation, it serves as an important backdrop for the more prominent discussions of the Spirit's work in the created order and public theology.

Concerning public theology specifically, Kuyper's life reveals that he was no mere theorist. He constantly sought ways to pursue public engagement, culminating in his election to prime minister of the Netherlands. While it is entirely possible to question the level of success Kuyper enjoyed at the height of his political powers, it cannot be denied that he attempted to embody his convictions concerning sphere sovereignty and governance according to the ordinances of creation.

In terms of his public theology, long before spelling out his perspective on Christian engagement, Kuyper articulated forms of his views on the divine ordinances and sphere sovereignty, particularly in the inaugural address of the Free University in 1880. At the pinnacle of his career, Kuyper articulated a form of public theology that clothed his deep Calvinist convictions in mythopoetic language, thus the labeling of his public theology as a rhetorical public theology. Though he was able to motivate the *kleine luyden* to public engagement, tensions can be found in Kuyper's public theology. Chief among these is the issue of antithesis and common grace. It can be argued that Kuyper's decision to emphasize Christian distinctiveness or the opportunities of common grace depended on the occasion, as can be seen, for example, in the Stone Lectures on science and art.

Kuyper's theology of common grace, fully trinitarian and undergirded by the Holy Spirit, serves as the ultimate basis for Kuyper's public theology. Chapter 3 demonstrated that Kuyper's doctrine of common grace was not an innovation by revealing that it was taught by John Calvin, though not with the level of detail seen in Kuyper. Though Kuyper spoke of Jesus Christ as the root and source of common grace, his discussion of the Spirit's work in creation displays language that is in some cases identical to a description of the function of common grace. This observation provides a way to speak of the Spirit as the dynamic element in common grace and to set forth a more fully trinitarian expression of the divine work in common grace. The Spirit's work of animating life, restraining sin, and moving creation to its *telos* is central to a theology of public engagement. There are concerns about Kuyper's doctrine of common grace, ranging from the relationship between creation and redemption to an excessive optimism regarding the development of society. As noted above, the infralapsarian view serves as one helpful approach to resolving the tensions, while S. U. Zuidema's resolution places common grace squarely under the domain of particular grace.

When considering the direction of the fourth chapter, some may argue that Kuyper's doctrines of cosmic pneumatology and common grace are sufficient only for certain cultures or epochs and thus best considered historically. To the contrary, a central conviction of chapter 4 is that it is in Kuyper's spirit to avoid mere repristination and to develop and recontextualize theology. While Kuyper was a late-nineteenth- to early-twentieth-century figure, his neo-Calvinism is in fact a catalyst for further theological development. While one may not find all of Kuyper's approach valuable, his cosmic pneumatology is generally useful and will prove indispensable as theologians continue to develop approaches to pneumatology for the future. One may need to reconfigure or restate aspects of his pneumatology as one understands more about the Spirit and creation, but one cannot ignore Kuyper's basic contribution. While a slowly expanding number of theologians has written about cosmic pneumatology, this increase has hardly made Kuyper or an approach rooted in his thought irrelevant or useless. There remains fertile ground in Kuyper's work for further development, particularly as we seek to understand how the Spirit is related to all aspects of a public theology.

With the assistance of figures such as John McIntyre, Arnold Van Ruler, and Richard Mouw, this work has attempted to set forth a fully trinitarian understanding of the Spirit's work in creation and history by searching for categories that have a specific pneumatological nuance and particular relevance for the Spirit's nonsalvific work in creation and common grace. The category of indwelling was found to be central, though more conservative than pantheistic or panentheistic approaches, as found in the work of Jürgen Moltmann, Geiko Müller-Fahrenholz, and Mark Wallace. From this pneumatological understanding, an approach to theology construed as the responsible stewardship of creation emerged. Such a pneumatological public theology ministers to the structures of creation as it attempts to respond to common grace, and it has a view toward constant revision in the social-architectural task, for there is the recognition that all social and cultural forms are relativized by their imperfection.

Questions remain, particularly in regard to the actual development of society. How does one develop society and culture in a way that encourages the flourishing of the entire created order? How does one appropriately discern the usefulness of technological advances, and how does one publicly make the case for such discernment so that something other than market forces has the final say? Ultimately, the question remains, How does one define and promote the common good, particularly in an era in which forms of commonness are under attack by the radicalization of postmodern thought? The answer so far is that we must seriously undertake the practice of discernment and tentatively assess whether social and cultural developments are truly the fruit of common grace.

Perpetuating a Legacy

How do we proceed at the dawn of the twenty-first century? Since Kuyper's era, the world has changed radically. How do we take the best of his legacy into a globalizing, pluralistic context? At the very least, we must recognize that the public theology we find in Kuyper eliminates any excuse for avoiding engagement with the public sphere. If indeed "every square inch" of creation is under the sovereign God who preserves it by the power of the Spirit, then Christians must winsomely and boldly enter the various areas of public life and undertake their stewardly tasks. Creation is good, though fallen, and remains ours to cultivate with the aim to produce forms of human flourishing that bring glory to God. This Kuyperian impulse remains.

Before proceeding further, we must face what happened after Kuyper's time. First, the progressive mind-set characteristic of Kuyper and his age was devastated by a twentieth century that revealed how "progress" can bequeath a Hitler, a Stalin, two world wars, and several smaller military conflicts (some specifically aimed at genocide, such as in Bosnia). While working on this book in Europe, I became aware of the specter that hovers like a dark cloud as a result of the world wars. With good reason, many Europeans are seemingly inoculated against the kind of optimism that preceded the twentieth century, and there is resistance to developments in culture and society that purport to be "new" ways forward to a better world.[1] I am

1. My thanks to George Harinck for making me aware of the European perspective.

an American, so optimism is easier for me than for my European counterparts. When America experienced devastation of a sort on September 11, 2001, the tragedy shattered a veneer of invincibility but not a belief in progress. There are, of course, laments about a decline in morality and civility, but there is no surrender to despair. On the other hand, a recognition of the tragedies of the previous century chasten any optimism that I would espouse. Nevertheless, theologically, the "spiritual" public theology rooted in Kuyper yields a cautious hope for cultivating a "better" future, even as eschatology makes us fully aware that paradise will come only by God's direct intervention at the consummation of all things.

A second issue that must be addressed is the "failure" of Kuyper. Many look at the Netherlands today and see Kuyper's project as quixotic. Some may even argue that Kuyper's effort was an ill-fated dream. While it is true that, if alive today, Kuyper might find the current state of the Netherlands troubling, it is unfair to regard the trajectory of the last six to seven decades as a final judgment on his project. Certainly, critics of neo-Calvinism will point to the recent dissolution of the Gereformeerde Kerken, the current state of the Vrije Universiteit, and the current state of pillarization (*verzuiling*) and suggest that a secularizing tendency was present all along in Kuyper's advocacy of public engagement. In my judgment, this criticism blames Kuyper for the manner in which his legacy was mishandled after his death, in a way similar to suggesting that South Africa's apartheid was always present in Kuyper's conception of sphere sovereignty (a spurious notion).

While it is certainly true that the legacy of neo-Calvinism has struggled in the Netherlands, it is mistaken to regard Kuyper as a failure. For one thing, he succeeded in giving a voice to a minority in the Netherlands, and he helped to produce viable institutions, even if they scarcely resemble his vision today. Furthermore, his influence in the United States and Canada has been fruitful in producing institutions that continue to thrive, and individuals are directly and indirectly influenced by his call for a comprehensive, world-engaging Christianity. Kuyper's perceived failure in the Netherlands cannot be a final judgment on his ideas. Are common grace, sphere sovereignty (even if modified), and antithesis theological concepts that belong in a museum of intellectual history? No, as the previous chapters have shown.

If Kuyper's legacy is viable, how do we carry it forward? First, we must reexamine the notion of "Kuyperianism." Scholars have often noted that Abraham Kuyper is regarded differently in the Netherlands than in the Western Hemisphere. In the United States and Canada particularly, Kuyper is often seen as a man of ideas rather than a man of history. In other words, to be "Kuyperian" in the Western Hemisphere often means that one finds affinity primarily with concepts such as common grace, sphere sovereignty, and antithesis. By itself this is not problematic, but it could yield an application of Kuyper's legacy that is little more than cutting and pasting his great ideas from his era into ours. The problem with such an approach is that Kuyper himself would never proceed in such a fashion. One of the reasons his opponents gave him the label "neo-Calvinist" was that he was undertaking a significant recontextualization of Reformed theology, and the result appeared so improvisational that it was perceived as significantly different from "true" Calvinism.[2] Neo-Calvinism resulted from Kuyper assessing his contemporary context and subsequently articulating a confessional, orthodox, comprehensive Christianity that compelled Christians to take to the public square. In Kuyper's era, issues such as the legacy of the French Revolution, the disenfranchisement of the *kleine luyden,* the secularization of the national church, and the looming specter of an all-encompassing state demanded the articulation of a public theology that addressed those particular challenges.

Kuyper's neo-Calvinism was the result less of his abilities as a systematic theologian than, to use Nicholas Wolterstorff's assessment, his intuitive genius[3] (Herman Bavinck was the superior systematic theologian). Kuyper certainly argued that principle must be placed against principle, and his focus on consistency does seem systematic, but one need look only at the episodic character of his writing and public addresses and the fact that he wrote considerably as a journalist in order to recognize that the character of his theology was a reflection of his intuitive genius. This is not to fault Kuyper but to point out that his work was produced in the midst of many ideological, eccle-

2. See John Bolt, *A Free Church, a Holy Nation: Abraham Kuyper's American Public Theology* (Grand Rapids: Eerdmans, 2001), 443–64.

3. See Nicholas Wolterstorff, "Abraham Kuyper's Model of a Democratic Polity for Societies with a Religiously Diverse Citizenry," in *Kuyper Reconsidered: Aspects of His Life and Work,* ed. Cornelis van der Kooi and Jan de Bruijn, VU Studies on Protestant History (Amsterdam: VU Uitgeverij, 1999), 205.

siological, and political battles. His primary aim was not to articulate a mammoth systematic text on a theology of public engagement but to develop and present a theologically grounded approach to public engagement for the various challenges of his day.

To be Kuyperian today, we must understand the challenges of our era (hopefully with even half the prescience Kuyper had about the future) and develop theologically grounded approaches to public engagement. With such a task at hand, how do we decide what to bring from Kuyper's era and what to leave in the past? If we would be *neo-Kuyperian,* what must we consider and how do we proceed?

Being Kuyperian means having a methodological approach as much as having a commitment to a conceptual apparatus. Among the issues that raise challenges for our era are globalization, the development and influence of technology, a more realized pluralism, the role of the market, catastrophic health crises such as AIDS in Africa, and ongoing struggles rooted in ethnic and class conflict. If we are to be like Kuyper in developing a robust public theology that responds to these challenges, we must do more than merely develop his principles. We must involve conversations outside our circles that yield intimate knowledge of the challenges at hand. In the best scenario, we will then be able to articulate how Christians can understand and practice a comprehensive Christianity that addresses the challenges and prepares us for the future.

Our approach will exhibit significant differences when compared to Kuyper's approach. As noted above, any optimism will be chastened by an awareness of recent history. We must resist triumphalism while maintaining hope that cultural and political forms of life can be developed that enhance human flourishing. Certainly, the newer Kuyperian contingent must be more multicultural. Spreading the influence of the best of Kuyper and developing his best impulses most fully will require the contribution of voices that Kuyper may not have expected. It will be impossible to respond to globalization, for example, without these voices.[4]

4. I am not here advocating an uncritical inclusion of each and every voice simply to be multicultural. Rather, I am suggesting that the myopia characteristic of our contextual embeddedness can best be countered by conversation with those from other contexts and that together we can help one another see clearly as we engage in a mutually critical discussion that will leave all parties better informed and able to practice their comprehensive Christianity more faithfully.

To be neo-Kuyperian, then, will require following Kuyper in his method of creatively responding to our context through the lens of a reformed Reformed faith. We must consider how to practice responsible stewardship of creation in an era of increasing complexity, even as globalization "shrinks" the planet. More fully aware of the Spirit's work in creation, we must heed the Spirit's impulse to "go public" in his power and to make fellow Christians aware that they too have been called to permeate every square inch of the world.

BIBLIOGRAPHY

Adams, James Luther. *On Being Human Religiously: Selected Essays in Religion and Society.* Edited by Max L. Stackhouse. Boston: Beacon, 1976.

Bavinck, Herman. "Common Grace." *Calvin Theological Journal* 24 (1989): 35–65.

———. "Creation or Development." *Methodist Review* 61 (1901): 849–74.

Begbie, Jeremy. *Voicing Creation's Praise: Toward a Theology of the Arts.* Edinburgh: T & T Clark, 1991.

Benne, Robert. *The Paradoxical Vision: A Public Theology for the Twenty-first Century.* Minneapolis: Fortress, 1995.

Berkhof, Hendrikus. *The Doctrine of the Holy Spirit.* Richmond: John Knox, 1964.

Berkouwer, G. C. *The Providence of God.* Grand Rapids: Eerdmans, 1952.

Bolt, John. "Abraham Kuyper as Poet: Another Look at Kuyper's Critique of the Enlightenment." In *Kuyper Reconsidered: Aspects of His Life and Work,* edited by Cornelis van der Kooi and Jan de Bruijn. Amsterdam: VU Uitgeverij, 1999.

———. "Common Grace, Theonomy, and Civic Good: The Temptations of Calvinist Politics." *Calvin Theological Journal* 33 (2000): 205–37.

———. "The Ecumenical Shift to Cosmic Pneumatology." *Reformed Review* 51 (Spring 1998): 255–70.

———. *A Free Church, a Holy Nation: Abraham Kuyper's American Public Theology.* Grand Rapids: Eerdmans, 2001.

Bratt, James D. "Abraham Kuyper, American History, and the Tensions of Neo-Calvinism." In *Sharing the Reformed Tradition: The Dutch-North American Exchange, 1846–1996,* edited by George Harinck and Hans Krabbendam. VU Studies on Protestant History. Amsterdam: VU Uitgeverij, 1996.

———, ed. *Abraham Kuyper: A Centennial Reader.* Grand Rapids: Eerdmans, 1998.

Calvin, John. *Commentaries on the Four Last Books of Moses Arranged in the Form of Harmony.* Vol. 3. Translated by Charles William Bingham. Grand Rapids: Baker, 1979.

———. *Commentary on the Book of the Prophet Isaiah.* Vol. 3. Translated by William Pringle. Grand Rapids: Baker, 1979.

———. *Commentary on the Gospel according to John.* Translated by William Pringle. Grand Rapids: Baker, 1979.

———. *Institutes of the Christian Religion.* Edited by John T. McNeill. Translated by Ford Lewis Battles. Philadelphia: Westminster, 1960.

Cunningham, David S. *These Three Are One: The Practice of Trinitarian Theology.* Malden, Mass.: Blackwell, 1998.

De Bruijn, Jan. "Abraham Kuyper as a Romantic." In *Kuyper Reconsidered: Aspects of His Life and Work,* edited by Cornelis van der Kooi and Jan de Bruijn. VU Studies on Protestant History. Amsterdam: VU Uitgeverij, 1999.

DeWitt, Calvin B. *Caring for Creation: Responsible Stewardship of God's Handiwork.* Grand Rapids: Baker, 1998.

Farley, Benjamin Wirt. *The Providence of God.* Grand Rapids: Baker, 1988.

Ferguson, Sinclair. *The Holy Spirit.* Downers Grove, Ill.: InterVarsity, 1996.

Geertz, Clifford. *The Interpretation of Cultures.* New York: Basic Books, 1973.

Gnanakan, Ken R. "The Holy Spirit, Creation, and New Creation." *Evangelical Review of Theology* 15 (April 1991): 101–10.

Grenz, Stanley J. *Renewing the Center: Evangelical Theology in a Post-theological Era.* Grand Rapids: Baker, 2000.

———. *Revisioning Evangelical Theology: A Fresh Agenda for the Twenty-first Century.* Downers Grove, Ill.: InterVarsity, 1993.

———, and John R. Franke. *Beyond Foundationalism.* Louisville: Westminster John Knox, 2001.

Gunton, Colin E. *Christ and Creation.* Grand Rapids: Eerdmans, 1992.

———. *The Doctrine of Creation.* Edinburgh: T & T Clark, 1997.

———. *The One, the Three, and the Many.* Cambridge: Cambridge University Press, 1993.

———. *The Promise of Trinitarian Theology.* Edinburgh: T & T Clark, 1991.

———. *The Triune Creator: A Historical and Systematic Study.* Edinburgh: Edinburgh University Press, 1998.

Hart, Hendrik, ed. *Rationality in the Calvinian Tradition.* Lanham, Md.: University Press of America, 1983.

Hauerwas, Stanley. *The Peaceable Kingdom: A Primer in Christian Ethics.* Notre Dame: University of Notre Dame Press, 1983.

Helm, Paul. *The Providence of God.* Downers Grove, Ill.: InterVarsity, 1994.

Henderson, R. D. "How Abraham Kuyper Became a Kuyperian." *Christian Scholars Review* 22 (September 1992): 22–35.

Heslam, Peter S. *Creating a Christian Worldview: Abraham Kuyper's Lectures on Calvinism.* Grand Rapids: Eerdmans, 1998.

Hoeksema, Herman. *The Protestant Reformed Churches in America: Their Origin, Early History, and Doctrine.* Grand Rapids: First Protestant Reformed Church, 1936.

Irvin, Dale T. *Christian Histories, Christian Traditioning: Rendering Accounts.* Maryknoll, N.Y.: Orbis, 1998.

Kasteel, P. *Abraham Kuyper.* Kampen: Kok, 1938.

Klapwijk, Jacob. "Antithesis and Common Grace." In *Bringing into Captivity Every Thought: Capita Selecta in the History of Christian Evaluations of Non-Christian Philosophy,* edited by Jacob Klapwijk, Sander Griffioen, and Gerben Groenewoud, 169–90. Lanham, Md.: University Press of America, 1991.

Kobes, Wayne A. "Sphere Sovereignty and the University: Theological Foundations of Abraham Kuyper's View of the University and Its Role in Society." Ph.D. diss., Florida State University, 1993.

Kooi, Cornelis van der. "A Theology of Culture. A Critical Appraisal of Kuyper's Doctrine of Common Grace." In *Kuyper Reconsidered: Aspects of His Life and Work,* edited by Cornelis van der Kooi and Jan de Bruijn. VU Studies on Protestant History. Amsterdam: VU Uitgeverij, 1999.

————, and Jan de Bruijn, eds. *Kuyper Reconsidered: Aspects of His Life and Work.* VU Studies on Protestant History. Amsterdam: VU Uitgeverij, 1999.

Kuiper, Dirk Th. *De Voormannen: een sociaal-wetenschappelijke studie over ideologie, konflikt en kerngroepvorming binnen de Gereformeerde wereld in Nederland tussen 1820 en 1930.* Meppel: Boom, 1972.

Kuiper, Herman. *Calvin on Common Grace.* Grand Rapids: Smitter Book Company, 1928.

Kuyper, Abraham. *Calvinism: Six Lectures Delivered in the Theological Seminary at Princeton.* New York: Revell, 1899.

————. *De Gemeene Gratie.* 2nd ed. 3 vols. Kampen: Kok, 1931–32.

————. *Principles of Sacred Theology.* Grand Rapids: Eerdmans, 1954.

————. *The Problem of Poverty.* Edited and with an introduction by James W. Skillen. Grand Rapids: Baker, 1991.

————. *Pro Rege, of het Koningschap van Christus.* 3 vols. Kampen: Kok, 1911–12.

————. *The Work of the Holy Spirit.* Translated by Hendrik de Vries. Grand Rapids: Eerdmans, 1900.

Langley, McKendree R. *The Practice of Political Spirituality: Episodes from the Public Career of Abraham Kuyper, 1879–1918.* Jordan Station, Ont.: Paideia, 1984.

Lindbeck, George. *The Nature of Doctrine: Religion and Theology in a Postliberal Age.* Philadelphia: Westminster, 1984.

Masselink, William. *General Revelation and Common Grace: A Defense of the Historic Reformed Faith.* Grand Rapids: Eerdmans, 1953.

McGoldrick, James E. *Abraham Kuyper: God's Renaissance Man.* Auburn, Mass.: Evangelical Press, 2000.

McIntyre, John. *The Shape of Pneumatology: Studies in the Doctrine of the Holy Spirit.* Edinburgh: T & T Clark, 1997.

Moltmann, Jürgen. *God in Creation: A New Theology of Creation and the Spirit of God.* Translated by Margaret Kohl. Minneapolis: Fortress, 1993.

—————. *The Source of Life: The Holy Spirit and the Theology of Life.* Minneapolis: Fortress, 1997.

—————. *The Spirit of Life: A Universal Affirmation.* Translated by Margaret Kohl. Minneapolis: Fortress, 1992.

Mouw, Richard. *He Shines in All That's Fair: Culture and Common Grace.* Grand Rapids: Eerdmans, 2001.

Müller-Fahrenholz, Geiko. *God's Spirit: Transforming a World in Crisis.* Geneva: WCC Publications, 1995.

Nash, James A. *Loving Nature: Ecological Integrity and Christian Responsibility.* Nashville: Abingdon, 1991.

Pinnock, Clark. *Flame of Love: A Theology of the Holy Spirit.* Downers Grove, Ill.: InterVarsity, 1997.

—————. "The Role of the Spirit in Creation." *Asbury Theological Journal* 52 (Spring 1997): 47–54.

Placher, William. *Unapologetic Theology: A Christian Voice in a Pluralistic Conversation.* Louisville: Westminster John Knox, 1989.

Praamsma, Louis. *Let Christ Be King: Reflections on the Life and Times of Abraham Kuyper.* Jordan Station, Ont.: Paideia, 1985.

Pronk, Cornelis. "Neo-Calvinism." *Reformed Theological Journal* 11 (1995): 42–56.

Puchinger, George. *Abraham Kuyper: De jonge Kuyper (1837–1867).* Franeker: T. Wever, 1987.

—————. *Abraham Kuyper: His Early Journey of Faith.* Edited by George Harinck. Translated by Simone Kennedy. Amsterdam: VU University Press, 1998.

Rasker, A. J. *De Nederlandse Hervormde Kerk vanaf 1795.* Kampen: Kok, 1974.

Richardson, Herbert W. *Toward an American Theology.* New York: Harper & Row, 1967.

Ridderbos, Simon Jan. *De Theologische Cultuurbeschouwing van Abraham Kuyper.* Kampen: Kok, 1947.

Romein, Jan. "Abraham Kuyper, 1837–1920: De klokkenist der kleine luyden." In Jan and Annie Romein, *Erflaters van onze beschaving,* 747–70. Amsterdam: Querido's, 1971.

Rullmann, J. C. *Kuyper-Bibliografie.* 3 vols. Kampen: Kok, 1940.

Skillen, James W., and Stanley W. Carlson-Thies. "Religion and Political Development in Nineteenth-Century Holland." *Publius* 12 (1982): 43–64.

Skillen, James W., and Rockne M. McCarthy, eds. *Political Order and the Plural Structure of Society.* Atlanta: Scholars Press, 1991.

Spykman, Gordon. *Reformational Theology: A New Paradigm for Doing Dogmatics.* Grand Rapids: Eerdmans, 1992.

Stackhouse, Max L. "Public Theology and Ethical Judgment." *Theology Today* 54 (July 1997): 165–79.

————. *Public Theology and Political Economy: Christian Stewardship in Modern Society.* Grand Rapids: Eerdmans, 1987.

————. "The Trinity as Public Theology: Its Truth and Justice for Free-Church, Noncredal Communities." In *Faith to Creed,* edited by S. Mark Heim. Grand Rapids: Eerdmans, 1991.

————, Peter L. Berger, Dennis P. McCann, and M. Douglas Meeks. *Christian Social Ethics in a Global Era.* Abingdon Press Studies in Christian Ethics and Economic Life 1. Nashville: Abingdon, 1995.

Stellingwerff, Johannes. *Dr. Abraham Kuyper en de Vrije Universiteit.* Kampen: Kok, 1987.

Stoeffler, F. Ernest. "Pietism: Its Message, Early Manisfestation, and Significance." *Covenant Quarterly* 32 (February/March 1976): 4–24.

Thiemann, Ronald F. *Constructing a Public Theology: The Church in a Pluralistic Culture.* Louisville: Westminster John Knox, 1991.

————. *Religion in Public Life: A Dilemma for Democracy.* Washington, D.C.: Georgetown University Press, 1996.

Tillich, Paul. *Systematic Theology.* Chicago: University of Chicago Press, 1963.

Tinder, Glenn. *The Political Meaning of Christianity: An Interpretation.* Baton Rouge: Louisiana State University Press, 1989.

Tracy, David. *The Analogical Imagination: Christian Theology and the Culture of Pluralism.* New York: Crossroad, 1981.

Vandenberg, Frank. *Abraham Kuyper.* Grand Rapids: Eerdmans, 1960.

Van Dyke, Harry. Review of *Creating a Christian Worldview: Abraham Kuyper's Lectures on Calvinism,* by Peter S. Heslam. *Calvin Theological Journal* 33 (November 1998): 506–7.

Vanhoozer, Kevin J., ed. *The Trinity in a Pluralistic Age: Theological Essays on Culture and Religion.* Grand Rapids: Eerdmans, 1997.

Van Ruler, Arnold A. *Calvinist Trinitarianism and Theocentric Politics: Essays toward a Public Theology.* Translated by John Bolt. Lewiston, N.Y.: Edwin Mellen, 1989.

Van Til, Cornelius. *Common Grace and the Gospel.* Phillipsburg, N.J.: Presbyterian & Reformed, 1972.

Van Til, Henry R. *The Calvinistic Concept of Culture.* 3rd ed. Philadelphia: Presbyterian & Reformed, 2001.

Veenhof, Jan. "A History of Theology and Spirituality in the Dutch Reformed Churches (1892–1992)." *Calvin Theological Journal* 28 (1993): 266–97.

Velema, W. H. *De Leer van de Heilige Geest bij Abraham Kuyper.* S'Gravenhage: Uitgeverij Van Keulen, 1957.

Wallace, Mark I. *Earth God: A Neopagan Christian Spirituality.* Forthcoming.

————. *Fragments of the Spirit: Nature, Violence, and the Renewal of Creation.* New York: Continuum, 1996.

Welker, Michael. *God the Spirit.* Translated by John Hoffmeyer. Minneapolis: Fortress, 1994.

Wintle, Michael J. *Pillars of Piety: Religion in the Netherlands in the Nineteenth Century, 1813–1901.* Hull, Eng.: Hull University Press, 1987.

Wolterstorff, Nicholas. *Until Justice and Peace Embrace.* Grand Rapids: Eerdmans, 1983.

Yoder, John Howard. *For the Nations: Essays Public and Political.* Grand Rapids: Eerdmans, 1997.

Yong, Amos. *Beyond the Impasse: Toward a Pneumatological Theology of Religions.* Grand Rapids: Baker Academic, 2002.

———. *Discerning the Spirit(s): A Pentecostal-Charismatic Contribution to Christian Theology of Religions.* Sheffield: Sheffield Academic Press, 2001.

Zizioulas, John. "Preserving God's Creation: Three Lectures on Theology and Ecology. *King's Theological Review* 12 (1989): 1–5, 41–45; and 13 (1990): 1–5.

Zuidema, S. U. "Common Grace and Christian Action in Abraham Kuyper." In *Communication and Confrontation,* edited by Gerben Groenewoud. Translated by Harry Van Dyke. Toronto: Wedge, 1972.

INDEX